EAT, DRINK & WAR EAGLE!

RECIPES FOR TAILGATING
ON THE PLAINS & AT HOME

PUBLISHED BY

BARKLEY & HOWLE
SPORTS PROMOTIONS

Published by

2545 Highland Avenue South
Birmingham, AL 35025

Design: Yellowhammer Marketing

Photo Stylist: Fonda Shaia
Food Stylist: Kathleen Kanen
Contributors: Bob Carlton
                Luke Anthony
                Pilar Taylor

ISBN 0-9769654-3-7

First Edition
Printed in the United States of America

Athletic Photography: Todd J. Van Emst
                         Athletic Dept. Photographer
                         Auburn University

The University name and logos featured on this product are registered trademarks of Auburn University.

Visit our website to submit recipes for the next edition or to order additional books: www.eatdrinkandwareagle.com

The crowd was riding high, with banners, cheers and toilet paper everywhere on the walk back from Jordan-Hare Stadium. September 14, 2002, and the Tigers had just tacked another win onto our ten-game record against Vanderbilt. Tailgaters all over Auburn began breaking out the grub with a vengeance. Kickoff had been at 11:30 today, leaving no time for lunch once we got our parking space, but the post-game feast was now at hand.

It had been a tough month for Auburn, schedule-wise. Today's game was one of four the Tigers played in 18 days. We'd shut out Western Carolina a week ago, but there were some doubts as to how long we could keep up the pace. The Auburn-Vanderbilt rivalry was still a good, old-fashioned Southern feud, all the way back to the glory days of Iron Mike Donahue and Shug Jordan.

Getting back to the truck, where we'd parked just north of the main campus, everyone was firing up the grills. A long row of cars, trucks and SUVs lined the street, each one sporting orange and blue. Pennants, caps and banners were all over the place. September on the Plains was still plenty hot before dusk, and I slid the blue cooler out of the truck. You could hear the thunk! thunk! thunk! as everybody popped open their coolers around.

After lighting the coals, I took a load off in a lawn chair. The air was shimmering over the closed grill as it heated up. We looked around as the sun moved down West. There was a delighted scream a few cars over – apparently, someone thought half a can of lighter fluid was a good idea. Maybe our neighbors on the other side had the right idea with their portable propane grill – less mess, and their food was nearly done. The spicy aroma of hot dogs and chili permeated the air around us; their grandkids were tossing the football back and forth on the grass nearby.

Still, there's no beating charcoal during football season on the Plains. It's primal instinct to cook with an open flame, reinforced by years of tailgating with Mom & Dad on this same campus, years before I attended. Tailgating's a sacred tradition, and some things just don't change. After a while, I got up and checked the coals – just about ready – and surveyed the massive victory party. It was like a wild hobo jungle, like an occupying army decked out in the school colors.

Someone turned on the stereo so we could listen to the post-game wrap-up. The ribs had been marinating for most of last night, and hissed as I laid them over the grill. I planted a pair of burgers in the little space I had left, and swung the lid shut. My old college roommate was muttering to himself, bent double over the side of the truck as he searched in vain for hot dogs he thought I packed. His two black labs had snatched his from the kitchen table early this morning.

Still, we had plenty to go around. Ribs, burgers, and a hefty row of side dishes lined up in rubber containers on the tailgate. No dessert, but that spread would be plenty and then some. I snuck around and reached into the little cooler, swiping another deviled egg from the covered tray. I had to feel around for a second. I wasn't the only one sneaking a few bites before dinner.

I heard an annoyed yell behind me, and gobbled the egg down on instinct.

"But, Graaaandpaaaaa!"

Looked like we weren't the only ones who'd forgotten something this morning. The kids next door had crowded around the grill, paper plates in hand, just to discover that they were minus hot dog buns. Ouch.

I thought about our current hot dog "situation", and glanced back at my wife and two friends. He was fussing with the radio dial, static crackling out in bursts, while the girls yelled at him to leave it alone. He finally ducked his head and backed off when Lisa started swatting him with her cap.

I found our unused bag of buns and, looking over at our neighbors, held it up in the air. The grandfather glanced over, ringed by young Tigers hopping up and down like hatchlings. We made eye contact, and I underhanded the bag over. The kids whirled around, jaws dropped. They were the picture of manners, and burst out with a schoolroom, "Thaaaank you!" in unison. Grandpa raised the buns in a salute, and I waved back.

The ribs smelled just about right. Someone had already taken the burgers off the grill, and I swung up the lid to check on them. A dark, fragrant cloud rolled out – upon closer inspection, they were just about perfect, thanks. I piled them out onto a plate, and we set up the spread on our fold-out table. Steaming ribs, burgers slathered in barbecue sauce, a somewhat-diminished deviled egg supply, corn on the cob, buttered rolls, and, thank the Lord, plenty of paper towels.

Everyone around us was digging in, too. The battle was over, the day was won, and the smells of tailgate barbecue were all around. War Eagle was proudly playing from someone's car stereo near-by. I poured myself a tall glass of sweet tea, lemons floating among the ice, and filled my plate. We had just sat down when I heard a sweet, Southern voice behind us.

"Um, 'scuse me?"

The grandmother next door had snuck up behind me, and I turned around. She'd probably brought back the leftover hot dog buns.

"Would y'all care for some brownies?"   Luke Anthony

Welcome to the first edition of **Eat, Drink and War Eagle!** We hope you enjoy this tailgating cookbook even more than we enjoyed putting it together. It wasn't easy sorting through all the mouth-watering recipes in the Southeast – but it sure was tasty. So fire up the grill, break out the lawn chairs and enjoy, to the tune of another historic season on the Plains!

War Eagle!

Frances Barkley, CEO and Mardis W. Howle, Jr., President of Barkley & Howle Sports Promotions

PRE-GAME: DRINKS 6
Pre-Game Warm-up

Mix the best drink for your tailgate party and get tips on managing all your ingredients on the trip into town. This section runs the gamut from flavored mojitos, to ice-cold homemade sweet tea, to warm mixed drinks like Irish Coffee.

1ST QUARTER: APPETIZERS 14
The Kick-Off

Find just what you need to wake up your appetite without putting it back to bed again. Even if it's just a snack for the road beforehand, or something to keep the starving hordes at bay while you grill your main course to perfection, here's a list of delicious tailgating appetizers you can nibble on for hours.

2ND QUARTER: SIDE DISHES 30
First & Ten

Even the best quarterback needs a tough offensive line for support. This section offers a wide range of side dishes to complement all your main courses. Everything from skillet-cooked veggies you simmer the night before to baked corn roasted on the grill.

3RD QUARTER: MAIN DISHES 48
Third & Long

Meat and fire. You know the staples – burgers, hot dogs, sausages, ribs . . . the list goes on and on and you know it by heart. Here's a practical guide to preparing, seasoning and cooking your main dishes to keep 'em coming back for more.

4TH QUARTER: DESSERT 72
Fourth Quarter's Ours

You got room for it, right? Assuming you haven't filled up on everything else (or even if you have), this section holds an impressive roster of sweets, pastries and other desserts to round off the meal. Cake, pie and brownies are just a few of the rewards you can dole out to those who kept their hands to themselves while you were cooking.

When you see this symbol in the recipes–go to the Resource section in the back of the book for ordering info.

PREGAME
d r i n k s

E veryone needs to keep cool under the hot southern sun and it's a must to give your guests something tall, cold and thirst-quenching to wash down their meal. In this section, find a cool batch of drinks to fend off the heat, whether you're tailgating or just enjoying the great outdoors. We've even thrown in a couple to help you get going in the morning with our delicious Bloody-Mary Bar. Be sure to have plenty of ice on hand—just because it's fall doesn't mean summer's quite over yet!

Left: Flavored Mojito *page 10*
Right: Tailgating Set-Up

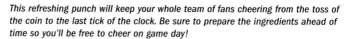

CHEERS!

This refreshing punch will keep your whole team of fans cheering from the toss of the coin to the last tick of the clock. Be sure to prepare the ingredients ahead of time so you'll be free to cheer on game day!

3 cups sugar

2 cups water

**1 (46-oz) can unsweetened pineapple juice
    or 1 (46-oz) bottle white grape juice**

1 (12-oz) can frozen orange juice or lemonade concentrate

4 quarts (16 cups/128-oz) ginger ale or lemon-lime soda, chilled

Lemon slices (optional)

Orange slices (optional)

At least one day ahead of time, combine the sugar and water in a saucepan, stirring to dissolve the sugar. Bring to a boil over medium heat, stirring constantly. Remove the pan from the heat and pour the sugar syrup into a container. Refrigerate until ready to mix the punch.

At least one day ahead of time, combine the pineapple or grape juice and frozen orange juice or lemonade concentrate in a large container; stir to mix well. Freeze until ready to mix the punch.

Just before serving, place the frozen juice mixture in a punch bowl or 2-3 large pitchers; add the sugar syrup and stir to mix. Pour in the ginger ale or lemon-lime soda; gently stir once or twice (the bubbles in the carbonated beverage will help mix the ingredients). Garnish with lemon and/or orange slices, if desired.

QUICK PUNCH

Gin, vodka, or rum can be added, if desired.

Ice scoop

Party ice in a bucket or other container

Large plastic cups

Bottles of regular or sparkling fruit juices, chilled

**Bottles or cans of plain or flavored ginger ale, lemon-lime soda, club soda, tonic
    water and other carbonated beverages**

Fruit slices or chunks

Maraschino cherries

Long party picks (to skewer the fruit for garnish)

Scoop the ice into a cup, fill the cup half-full with one or more fruit juices and add enough carbonated beverage to fill the cup; there's no need to stir—the bubbles will mix the ingredients. Garnish with fruit on a pick.

MINTED PICK-ME-UP ICED TEA

Make this recipe at least a day ahead of time, pour it into a clean gallon jug and refrigerate until ready to serve. For an extra flavor boost, use a spiced tea.

3/4 cup lemon juice
8 tea bags
10-12 sprigs mint
2 cups boiling water
2-2 1/2 cups sugar
2 quarts cold water
1 cup orange juice
Additional sprigs mint (optional)

Boil the sugar in 2 cups water with mint for 5 minutes to make mint syrup. Strain the liquid and set aside.

Pour 1 quart boiling water over the tea bags and steep for 5 minutes. Mix together the mint syrup, tea, lemon and orange juices. Dilute to one gallon.

Serve over ice and garnish with additional sprigs of mint, if desired.

FRUITY BUBBLES

3 quarts unsweetened tea
1/2 - 1 cup sugar
1 (12-oz) can frozen lemonade or limeade concentrate
1 quart (4 cups) ginger ale or lemon-lime soda, chilled
Lemon slices (optional)
Lime slices (optional)

Combine all of the ingredients in a punch bowl or large pitchers; gently stir once or twice (the bubbles in the carbonated beverage will help mix the ingredients). Serve over ice and garnish with lemon and/or lime slices, if desired.

SPICED CIDER

You can add flavored rum to this recipe, if desired.

Cinnamon, to taste
Nutmeg, to taste
3 gallons cider
Cinnamon sticks (optional)

A day ahead of time, add cinnamon and nutmeg to taste to each gallon of cider; refrigerate overnight. Serve cold over ice or heat just before serving; garnish with cinnamon sticks, if desired.

"I don't like cigars, but I'm going to smoke this one."

-Auburn tight end Derrick Dorn after the Tigers thumped Bama 22-14 in 1993.

GIN SOUR
3-oz gin
1-oz freshly squeezed lemon juice
1 teaspoon sugar syrup
Lemon or orange slice
Maraschino cherry

Combine the gin, lemon juice and sugar syrup in a shaker half filled with ice; shake vigorously and strain into a chilled sour glass. Garnish with either a lemon or orange slice and a maraschino cherry.

ORANGE BLOSSOM
1 1/2-oz gin
1-oz freshly squeezed orange juice
Orange slice

Combine the gin and orange juice in a shaker half filled with ice; shake vigorously and strain into a chilled cocktail glass. Garnish with the slice of orange.

FLAVORED MOJITOS
Flavored rum replaces light rum in this updated version of the classic rum, lime and mint drink.
12 mint leaves
1/2 lime
2-3 teaspoons sugar
1-2-oz flavored rum of choice
Club soda
Sprig of mint
Lime wedge

Crush the mint leaves with a pestle and mortar and scrape into a collins glass (you can crush the mint with a long-handled spoon in the bottom of the serving glass if the glass is heavy enough).

Squeeze the juice from the lime into the serving glass. Drop the squeezed lime into the glass and add the sugar; muddle (stir) until well mixed.

Fill the glass with ice. Pour the rum over the ice and top with a splash of club soda. Garnish with the mint sprig and lime wedge.

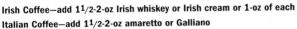

PRE-GAME
drinks

BASIC FLAVORED-COFFEE

For an early tailgate brunch, start off with these coffee drinks.

5-6-oz freshly brewed coffee
1¹/2-2-oz alcoholic beverage of choice
Whipped sweetened heavy cream (optional)

Warm a coffee glass or mug by filling it with hot water ahead of time; pour out the water when you are ready to mix the drink.

Pour the hot coffee into the warm serving glass; add the alcoholic beverage of choice and stir gently to mix. Top with whipped cream if desired.

Irish Coffee—add 1¹/2-2-oz Irish whiskey or Irish cream or 1-oz of each
Italian Coffee—add 1¹/2-2-oz amaretto or Galliano
Jamaican Coffee—add 1¹/2-2-oz rum or 1-oz rum and 1-oz coffee-flavored liqueur or brandy
Mexican Coffee—add 1¹/2-2-oz tequila or 1-oz tequila and 1-oz coffee liqueur
Russian Coffee—add ¹/2-oz each vodka, hazelnut-flavored liqueur and coffee-flavored liqueur

BRANDY SLUSH

7 cups water
2 cups sugar
4 tea bags
2 cups boiling water
1 (16-oz) can frozen lemonade concentrate
1 (16-oz) can frozen orange juice concentrate
1 pint peach brandy
Lemon-lime soda, ginger ale, or other carbonated beverage

Pour the 7 cups of water into a saucepan; add the sugar and bring to a boil over medium heat, stirring constantly. Remove from the heat and let cool.

Place the tea bags in a small bowl; add the 2 cups of boiling water and let stand for 10 minutes. Remove the tea bags and pour the tea into a large container; add the sugar water and stir to mix. Add the concentrates and brandy; stir to mix well, cover and place in the freezer until ready to serve. Spoon the frozen mixture into serving glasses and top with the carbonated beverage.

Before the 1972 game, Alabama Coach Paul Bryant made the mistake of calling Auburn a "cow college." As Bryant and his players would soon discover, those cows could play football, too. In one of the most glorious afternoons in Auburn history, the Tigers topped the Tide 17-16 that year.

"When those cows get mad they kick," Auburn running back Terry Henley said after the game. "I know, 'cause I've been around 'em all my life. "There won't be enough people going back to Auburn to milk them tonight."

SANGRIA

Adapt this recipe using your favorite fruits, beverages and flavors–sliced strawberries and kiwi, fresh blueberries and raspberries, gin, rum, ginger ale, citrus soda, or lime juice.

Party ice

1/2 cup brandy

1/4 cup Cointreau

4 cups red wine

Juice of 3 lemons

Sugar, to taste

2 thinly sliced oranges

1 thinly sliced lemon

1/4 cup seeded sweet cherries

1 cup sliced fresh or canned peaches

Fill a large pitcher half full with the ice; pour the brandy, Cointreau, red wine and lemon juice over the ice and stir to mix. Add sugar to taste and stir to mix. Either serve immediately or chill;. Just before serving add the fruit.

We owe this game to one person and that's Coach Pat Dye."

–Terry Bowden, who took over when Dye retired, addressing the Auburn crowd following the 22-14 win over Alabama in 1993.

BLOODY MARY BAR

Encouraging guests to serve themselves is simple. Just set up a Bloody Mary bar! All you have to do is put the ingredients on a serving table along with directions for mixing the drink "from scratch" (see the traditional recipe below, including the nonalcoholic "Virgin" Mary version) or with a ready-to-use mixer (see product labels). Also put a shaker (for people who prefer their drink shaken rather than stirred), a jigger/pony or standard measuring glass, measuring cups and spoons and other basic bar tools on the table.

Stock your Bloody Mary bar with:
Vodka, Gin, Rum, Tequila

A variety of Bloody Mary mixers ranging from mild and smooth to hot and spicy

And/Or

Tomato juice, freshly squeezed lemon juice, Tabasco sauce, Worcestershire sauce

Celery salt, dried or fresh chopped dill, white pepper, black pepper

Horseradish, other desired seasonings

TRADITIONAL BLOODY MARY

Omit the vodka to make the nonalcoholic "Virgin" Mary.

4-6-oz tomato juice

2-oz vodka

1-1 1/2 teaspoons lemon juice

1/4 teaspoon Worcestershire sauce

Several dashes of Tabasco sauce

1 teaspoon freshly grated horseradish squeezed dry, if desired

1/2-1 teaspoon dried or fresh chopped dill
1-2 pinches celery salt
Pinch of white or black pepper
Celery stalk

Combine all of the ingredients except the celery stalk in a shaker with ice; shake gently. Pour (strain, if desired) the mixed drink into a serving glass; garnish with a celery stalk.

Frozen Margarita

BASIC MARGARITA
1 1/2-oz white or gold tequila
1/2-oz triple sec or other orange-flavored liqueur
Juice of 1/2 large lime

Pour all of the ingredients into a shaker; fill the shaker with ice and shake vigorously. Strain the mixed drink into a chilled, salted serving glass.

FROZEN MARGARITA
2 cups cracked ice
1 1/2-oz white or gold tequila
1/2-oz triple sec or other orange-flavored liqueur
1-oz lime or lemon juice

Place the ice in a heavy-duty blender and pour in the remaining ingredients. Blend until slushy but still firm; pour the mixed drink into a chilled, salted serving glass.

An undefeated Auburn team trailed Alabama 14-5 in the middle of the third quarter at Jordan-Hare Stadium. The Tigers had the ball fourth and 15 on the Tide 35. Too far to kick a field goal. Too close to punt. Tiger coach Terry Bowden decided to go for it all. But on the play before, senior quarterback Stan White injured his knee and had to leave the game. White's back-up, Patrick Nix, grabbed his helmet and hurried onto the field. In the huddle, Nix relayed the play: 78 Stay Z Takeoff, a deep, stop-and-go pass route down the sideline. He looked at receiver Frank Sanders. "Just catch it," Nix said. "You get it up there and I'll catch it," Sanders told him. He did, out-leaping Alabama defender Tommy Johnson near the goal line and diving into the end zone. Just like that it was 14-12 and momentum was on the Tigers' side. Alabama would never score again. Auburn would score 10 more in the fourth quarter to win 22-14, capping an 11-0 season and ending a three-game losing streak to Alabama. And 78 Z Stay Takeoff, lofted by a quarterback who didn't even have time for a warm-up throw before he was thrust into the action, was the play of the game. "I guess you call it a fairy tale," Bowden said. "Isn't that what you call it?

THE KICK-OFF

1ST QUARTER
a p p e t i z e r s

t never fails – the instant you start cooking, everyone starts paying attention to their appetite. Put a stop to the cries of "Is it ready yet?" by serving up some appetizers. They're quick, easy and just the thing to wake up your appetite without putting it back to bed again. Black-Eyed Pea Dip, Touchdown Wings and other tasty nibblers will hit the spot and make great snacks for any time of the day! These appetizers are just what you need to quiet the rumbling until everyone's ready to dig in.

Left: Gazpacho Dip *page 16*

Right: Spicy Spiced Nuts *page 27* are a perennial Southern favorite.

CHEESE-CHILI LOGS

1/2-lb processed cheese, softened
1 (4-oz) package cream cheese, softened
1 tablespoon minced onion
2-3 cloves garlic, minced
1/4 teaspoon seasoned salt
1/4 teaspoon Worcestershire sauce
Chili powder, to taste

Combine all of the ingredients except the chili powder in a bowl; mix well. Divide the mixture into four parts, and shape each part into a 1 1/2-inch-thick log. Lightly roll each log in the chili powder, and wrap in waxed paper; place in either the refrigerator or freezer. When ready to serve, remove as many logs as desired, and let them warm to room temperature; cut the logs into slices, and serve with round crackers.

"I can look back 20 years from now and say we started a tradition and I was part of it."

–Defensive tackle Gerald Williams, after Auburn beat Alabama 23-20 in 1983, its second win in a row after losing nine straight to the Tide.

GAZPACHO DIP

3 tablespoons oil
1 1/2 tablespoons cider vinegar
1 teaspoon salt
1 teaspoon garlic salt
1/4 teaspoon pepper
1 can chopped black olives, with liquid
1 (4-oz) can chopped green chiles, with liquid
3 tomatoes, chopped
5 green onions, finely chopped
Cilantro, finely chopped

Whisk oil and vinegar; add the next three ingredients, whisking more. Combine the olives, chilies, tomatoes and green onions in a medium bowl and pour the liquid over them. Chill for several hours. When ready to serve, mix with a bit of chopped cilantro to taste. Serve with tortilla chips.

CHEESE SPREAD

2 -lbs grated sharp cheddar cheese
1 clove garlic
1 teaspoon salt
1 teaspoon powdered mustard
🌶 3 teaspoons Porky's Bellycheer Worcestershire Fire Sauce
Dash of cayenne pepper
Horseradish, to taste
1 cup beer

Combine the cheese and garlic together in a bowl or food processor; process until smooth. Add the remaining ingredients and stir gently to mix; additional beer may be added if needed for softer consistency. Store in the refrigerator.

"On that last drive, (Ben) Tamburello, said, 'This is it; we got to go.' And you could see it in our eyes. We weren't going to fail."

–Running back Brent Fullwood, on Auburn's final, 67-yard drive to beat Alabama 21-17 in 1983.

CHUTNEY-NUT STUFFED BRIE

16 SERVINGS

Serve this appetizer with assorted crackers and red and green seedless grapes.

2 (8-oz, 4^1/2-inch-round) Brie wheels
1 (8-oz) package cream cheese, softened
2 tablespoons butter, softened
2 tablespoons prepared chutney
1/8 teaspoon pepper
1/2 cup toasted sliced or slivered almonds, divided
2 tablespoons chopped parsley, divided
Grapes
Crackers

Cut the Brie in half horizontally; place the bottom 2 halves on a serving plate and set the top half aside.

Combine the cream cheese and butter in a bowl; beat with an electric mixer at medium high speed until fluffy. Add the chutney and pepper; continue beating until well mixed.

Spread half of the cream cheese mixture on the bottom layers of Brie; sprinkle with half of the almonds and half of the parsley. Top with the remaining halves of Brie and press lightly. Spread the remaining cream cheese mixture evenly over the tops and sprinkle with the remaining almonds and parsley. Cover and refrigerate for at least 1 hour.

CHEDDAR CHEESE DIP

1 1/2 CUPS

You can add up to an additional 1/4 cup of beer to make a thinner dip. If you make the recipe ahead of time, refrigerate the dip and reheat it in the microwave, 30 seconds at a time, stirring after each interval until it is hot. The mellow, rich cheddar flavor makes it perfect for both chips and fresh vegetables.

2 tablespoons butter
1/4 cup chopped onion
1 cup flat beer
1 (3-oz) package cream cheese, softened
4 -oz shredded cheddar cheese
Dash paprika
Dash cayenne pepper (or more, to taste)

Melt the butter in a saucepan over medium high heat; add the onion and sauté for 2 minutes or until the onion is soft. Add the beer and bring the mixture to a boil; remove the pan from the heat. Add the remaining ingredients and stir gently until the cheese has completely melted. Sprinkle with additional paprika for garnish. Serve warm.

POULTRY PARTY ROLL

4-6 SERVINGS

1 (3-oz) package cream cheese, softened
3 tablespoons margarine, melted and divided
2 cups cubed cooked turkey or chicken
1/4 teaspoon salt
1/8 teaspoon pepper
2 tablespoons milk
1 tablespoon chopped chives or onion
1 tablespoon chopped pimiento (optional)
1 (8-oz) can crescent rolls
3/4 cup crushed seasoned croutons

Preheat oven to 350°.

Combine the cream cheese and 2 tablespoons of the melted butter in a bowl; blend until smooth. Add the turkey, salt, pepper, milk, chives, and pimiento (if desired); mix well.

Press the edges of the crescent roll dough together on a foil-lined baking pan, forming a rectangle. Spoon the cream cheese-turkey mixture down the middle; fold in the ends and sides, and press to seal. Brush the remaining melted butter over the top, and sprinkle with the crushed croutons. Bake for 20-25 minutes or until golden brown. Remove from the oven; either serve immediately, or let cool, and serve at room temperature.

MEXICAN SKILLET DIP

2-lbs ground chuck
3 cans refried beans
1 large can tomato sauce
2 bottles spicy-hot ketchup
3 teaspoons chili powder
Grated cheddar cheese, to taste
1 can chopped olives, drained
Green onions
Tortilla chips

Cook the ground chuck in a skillet over medium heat until browned and crumbly; drain and set aside. Combine the beans, tomato sauce, ketchup, and chili powder in a skillet or wok, and heat until warm; add the cooked ground chuck, and mix well.

Just before serving, sprinkle the grated cheese and chopped olives over the top; garnish with the whole green onions. Serve warm with tortilla chips.

SALMON SUPREME SPREAD

1 (8-oz) package cream cheese, softened
1/3 cup heavy cream
2 green onions, minced
1/8 teaspoon Tabasco sauce
1 teaspoon lemon juice
4-5-oz smoked salmon, shredded
2 tablespoons salmon caviar (optional)

Combine the cream cheese and heavy cream in a bowl; beat until smooth. Add the green onions, Tabasco sauce, and lemon juice; stir to mix well. Fold in the salmon and caviar (if desired), and refrigerate. Serve with bread and/or crackers.

PINEAPPLE-CREAM CHEESE SPREAD

1 (8-oz) package cream cheese, softened
1/4 cup diced pineapple
2 tablespoons finely chopped pecans
1 teaspoon vanilla extract

Combine all of the ingredients in a bowl; stir to mix well, and refrigerate. To serve, spread on date-nut or whole-wheat bread.

One year after making his freshman debut with "Bo Over the Top," Vincent "Bo" Jackson returned for an encore against Alabama in 1983. The rain came down in sheets. Tornadoes threatened. But on this day, you didn't need a weatherman to know which way Bo was going. All Jackson did that dreary, wet afternoon was race for 256 yards and score two touchdowns on lightning-bolt runs of 69 and 71 yards each. "Bo his put his name into Auburn history," his coach, Pat Dye, said. "I'd hate to think where we'd be if Bo wasn't in our backfield today," quarterback Randy Campbell added. "There's something about Alabama that pumps him up."

CHILLED ASPARAGUS

1 bunch asparagus
1 (0.6 -oz) package Onion or Italian Dressing Mix
1 tablespoon coarse sea salt

Bring water to a boil in a shallow pan; drop in the asparagus and boil for 3 minutes; drain and immediately place in a flat (3-quart) container. Cover the asparagus with ice and refrigerate for 30 minutes. Remove the asparagus from the ice and pat dry. Wipe the container; place the dry asparagus into the container and sprinkle the dressing mix over the top. Refrigerate until serving time.

SPICY ITALIAN SQUARES

1-lb spicy sausage
1/4 -lb pepperoni, cut into small pieces
1/4 -lb salami, cut into small pieces
4-6-oz mozzarella cheese, cut into small pieces
1/2 cup grated Romano cheese
1/2 cup grated Parmesan cheese
6 eggs, beaten

Preheat the oven to 350°. Grease an 8-inch square baking pan.

Cook the sausage until crumbly; drain well and place in a bowl. Add the remaining ingredients and mix well. Pour into the prepared pan; bake for 25-30 minutes or until the top is brown. Let cool; cut into 1-inch squares.

BACON'N'EGG DIP

ABOUT 3 CUPS

You can make this recipe the day before and store it in the refrigerator.

1 (8-oz) package cream cheese, softened
4 hard boiled eggs, finely chopped
4 strips bacon, cooked until crisp, drained, and crumbled
2 tablespoons dill pickle relish
1/2 green pepper, seeded and chopped
1/2 cup thinly sliced green onions with tops
1 tablespoon milk
Salt
Pepper

Stir milk into the softened cream cheese. Combine the cream cheese, eggs, bacon, pickle relish, green pepper, and onions in a bowl; stir gently until well mixed. Add salt and pepper to taste. Cover tightly, and refrigerate for at least 2 hours. Serve with crisp broccoli, carrots and cauliflower.

BUFFALO HOT WINGS

2-lbs chicken wings
🏈 8 tablespoons Tennessee Red Lightnin'
1/3 stick melted butter or margarine
1 tsp. salt
🏈 Bellycheer BBQ SeasonZing & Rub
Bleu cheese dressing
Celery sticks

Cut wings at joint and discard tips. Wash thoroughly and pat dry.
Sprinkle with Bellycheer BBQ SeasonZing
& Rub and gently rub in. Marinate in
refrigerator for at least 30 minutes or over
night.

Either deep fry at 400° for 10-12 minutes
until crisp, OR bake at 425° in an oven for
30 minutes, turn and bake additional 30 minutes.

Mix salt, butter and Tennessee Red
Lightnin'. Put cooked wings into colander.
Pour sauce over wings while hot, tossing to
cover all. Serve with additional hot sauce,
bleu cheese, dressing and ice cold celery
sticks.

RYE SPREAD

ENOUGH SPREAD FOR 4 LOAVES OF PARTY
RYE ROUNDS

2 2/3 cups sour cream
2 2/3 cups mayonnaise
12-oz chopped corned beef
4 tablespoons minced onion
4 tablespoons chopped fresh parsley
4 teaspoons dill seed
3-4 teaspoons Beau Monde seasoning

Combine all of the ingredients in a large bowl; mix thoroughly, cover,
and refrigerate overnight. Serve with rye rounds.

CHILI-CHEESE SQUARES
2 (4-oz) cans green chilies
1 (10-oz) package sharp cheddar cheese, grated
6 eggs, beaten
2 tablespoons taco seasoning mix

Preheat oven to 275°. Grease a 9 x 13-inch glass pan.

Arrange the chilies in the bottom of the prepared pan; sprinkle with the cheese. Mix the taco seasoning mix into the eggs and pour the eggs evenly over the top. Bake for 45 minutes; remove the pan from the oven and cut into squares. Serve either hot or cold.

STUFFED EGGS WITH CRABMEAT
12 hard boiled eggs
1 cup crabmeat
1 cup celery, finely chopped
1 tablespoon French salad dressing
2 tablespoons finely chopped green pepper
1/3 cup sour cream

Peel the eggs and cut them in half lengthwise; place them on a serving plate or tray. Remove the yolks and mash them in a small bowl; stir in the remaining ingredients and mix well. Stuff the egg halves with the filling mixture. Place in an airtight container, seal and refrigerate until ready to serve.

"I've cried until I can't cry any more."

–Auburn lineman Mac Lorendo, after the Tigers blocked two punts to pull off that incredible 17-16 upset of Alabama in 1972.

HOMEMADE BOURSIN CHEESE
This tastes best when made ahead of time; it will keep up to 10 days in the refrigerator. To make a dip, add 1/2 cup sour cream to the cheese spread.
8-oz cream cheese, softened
1 clove garlic, crushed
2 teaspoons minced fresh parsley
1/2 teaspoon chopped basil leaves
2 tablespoons chopped chives
1 tablespoon dry white vermouth
Pinch of pepper

Combine the cream cheese and garlic in a bowl; blend well. Add the remaining ingredients and blend well. Store the spread in an airtight container in the refrigerator.

FIRST DOWN DIP

1 grilled chicken breast, diced
2 cups chived cream cheese, softened
1 cup cooked black beans
1/2 cup chopped green onions
1/2 cup diced tomatoes
1 tablespoon sour cream
1 tablespoon chopped fresh basil
1 teaspoon chopped garlic
🏈 Porky's Bellycheer Jalapeño Pepper Sauce
Seasoning salt, to taste
1 cup mixed cheddar/Monterey Jack cheese

Combine all of the ingredients except the cheddar/Monterey Jack cheese in a bowl; mix well. Sprinkle the cheese over the top; refrigerate if desired. Serve the dip at room temperature or chilled with blue corn chips and tortillas. Store leftover dip in the refrigerator.

FRESH SALSA

ABOUT 1 1/2 CUPS
3 tomatoes, finely chopped
1/2 cup chopped onion
4-6 fresh serrano chili peppers, seeded and finely chopped
1 tablespoon finely chopped fresh cilantro
2 teaspoons salt
2 teaspoons fresh lime juice

Combine all of the ingredients in a bowl; stir to mix well. Let stand for at least 1 hour before serving.

It was 1986, the last Saturday in November and Auburn trailed Alabama 17-14 with less than a minute remaining on the Legion Field clock. Pat Dye jumped up and down on the Auburn sideline, frantically trying to call a timeout. But Tiger quarterback Jeff Burger didn't see his coach. "Eighteen Reverse Left!" Burger shouted. Wide receiver Lawyer Tillman knew something was wrong. "Eighteen Reverse Left!" Burger shouted again as the players ran into position. But the play was designed for backup wide receiver Scott Bolton, not Tillman, who had never run the reverse before. Bolton wasn't even on the field. Tillman tried to call timeout, too, but before he could, Burger had already taken the snap and pitched the ball to tailback Tim Jessie, who swept right and then handed it off to Tillman going the other way. Aided by a block from Burger, Tillman danced around the Alabama defenders and dashed seven yards for the winning touchdown with 32 seconds to go, sealing a 21-17 Auburn victory and making Tillman a folk hero. In the Auburn locker room afterward, Dye gave Tillman a kiss on the cheek. "That's the first reverse I ever run in my life," Tillman said. "I wasn't supposed to be in there."

CREAMY SPINACH-LEEK DIP

3 1/2 CUPS

You can make this recipe a day ahead and store it in the refrigerator. Serve the dip with bread, crackers and/or vegetable slices and chunks; or hollow out the center of a round loaf of bread (reserve the removed bread), fill the bread shell with the dip and serve with pieces of the reserved bread and vegetables.

1 tablespoon olive oil
1 cup thinly sliced leek (about 1 medium)
2 cloves garlic, minced
8-oz cream cheese, softened
1/2 cup sour cream
1/4 cup mayonnaise
1/2 teaspoon white vinegar
1/2 teaspoon salt
1/4 teaspoon ground black pepper
1 (10-oz) package frozen spinach, thawed and drained
1/4 teaspoon dried dill
1 (8-oz) can water chestnuts, drained and chopped

Heat the oil in a skillet over medium high heat. Add the sliced leek and sauté 8 minutes or until soft and just beginning to brown. Add the garlic and sauté an additional 30 seconds. Remove the skillet from the heat and let the leek mixture cool completely.

Combine the leek mixture, cream cheese, sour cream, mayonnaise, vinegar, salt and pepper in a food processor; process until smooth. Add the spinach and dill and pulse just until combined; add the water chestnuts and stir to mix. Cover tightly and refrigerate until ready to serve.

HEN AND HEIFER

1 (6.5-oz) can chunk chicken
1 (8-oz) package cream cheese
1 (3-oz) package cream cheese
1/2 cup mayonnaise
1/2 teaspoon garlic or onion salt
1/2 cup pecan pieces
1/2 cup pecans, finely chopped

Combine the chicken, 2 packages of cream cheese, mayonnaise, garlic or onion salt, and pecan pieces in a bowl; mix well. Shape the mixture into a ball or log on waxed paper; place on a plate or tray, and refrigerate. Just before serving roll the ball or log in the finely chopped pecans.

CREAM CHEESE-OLIVE SPREAD

ABOUT 1 1/2 CUPS

2 (3-oz) packages cream cheese, softened
2 tablespoons mayonnaise
1/8 teaspoon pepper
4 small onions, finely chopped
1/2 cup chopped pimento-stuffed olives

Combine the cream cheese, mayonnaise, and pepper in a bowl; beat until smooth. Stir in the onions and olives.

FRANCES' FETA CHEESE DIP

You can find zahtar spice at Middle Eastern food stores.

1 cup feta cheese, crumbled
1 cup sour cream
2 tablespoons lemon juice
2 tablespoons chopped green onions
1 tablespoon chopped parsley
2 cloves garlic, pressed
1 teaspoon zahtar spice
Dash freshly ground pepper

Combine all of the ingredients in a bowl; mix well, and refrigerate. Serve with crackers and/or raw vegetables.

TOUCHDOWN WINGS

1 cup soy sauce
1 cup grapefruit juice
1/4 cup hoisin sauce
🐖 1/4 cup Porky's Historic Lynchburg Jalapeño Ketchup
1/4 cup rice wine vinegar
1/2 cup sesame seeds
1/4 cup light brown sugar
5 halved cloves garlic
3 tablespoons ground ginger
24 chicken wings

Combine all of the ingredients except the chicken in a large, self-sealing, heavy-duty plastic bag; seal the bag and shake to mix well. Add the chicken and refrigerate overnight. Cook on a hot grill until brown (about 5-7 minutes per side).

Clockwise from top left:
Creamy Spinach-Leek Dip,
page 24, Chutney-Stuffed
Brie, *page 17,* Sangria,
page 12, Cheddar-Cheese
Dip, *page 18*

JALAPEÑO SHRIMP DIP

2 (7-oz) cans shrimp, drained
1¹/2 cups mayonnaise
1 clove garlic, crushed
1 small onion, grated
1 cup grated sharp cheddar cheese
🏈 1 teaspoon Porky's Bellycheer Jalapeño Pepper Sauce
Sliced jalapeños

Combine all of the ingredients in a bowl; stir to mix well. Cover
tightly and refrigerate until serving time. Garnish with sliced jalapeños
and serve with crackers.

SPICY-SPICED NUTS

2 CUPS

You can make this recipe a day ahead.

1 1/2 tablespoons butter
3/4 teaspoon ground cumin
1 tablespoon brown sugar
1 tablespoon white sugar
1 teaspoon salt
1/8 teaspoon red pepper
1/8 teaspoon black pepper
2 cups unsalted nuts (pecans, cashews and/or peanuts)

Preheat the oven to 300°. Line a baking pan with foil.

Melt the butter in a large saucepan over medium high heat. Add the cumin, brown sugar, white sugar, salt, red pepper and black pepper; cook 4 minutes or until the sugars dissolve, stirring constantly. Remove the pan from the heat; add the nuts, stirring gently to coat.

Arrange the nuts evenly on the prepared pan; bake for 15 minutes, stirring twice. Remove from the oven and let cool completely. Store in an airtight container.

HORSERADISH DIP

1 (8-oz) package cream cheese
1/3 cup sour cream
3 tablespoons heavy cream
Juice of 1/2 lemon
2 tablespoons horseradish
1 teaspoon Creole mustard
3-4 dashes hot pepper sauce
Salt, to taste
Pepper, to taste
3 tablespoons finely chopped parsley

Combine all of the ingredients except the parsley in a bowl; beat until fluffy. Refrigerate the mixture; just before serving, sprinkle the parsley over the top. Serve with raw vegetables.

First Down Menu

Creamy Spinach-Leek Dip served with bread, crackers and/or vegetable slices and chunks (p24)

✕

Spicy-Spiced Nuts (p27)

✕

Sirloin Chili (p61)

✕

Buttermilk-Scallion Cornbread (p33)

✕

Hearty Green Salad with Mandarin Oranges and Goat Cheese (p36)

✕

Pumpkin-Walnut Cake (p74)

BE-DEVILED EGGS

24 DEVILED EGG HALVES

It is best to make this recipe the day you plan to serve the eggs.
Travel tip: *Fill the egg white shells with the yolk mixture, but do not garnish. Reassemble the eggs, cut sides touching; wrap each reassembled egg in plastic wrap, place in an airtight container and store in a cooler until serving time. Just before serving, unwrap the eggs and pull apart the halves; smooth the top of the filling with a knife or the back of a spoon and garnish with the pecans.*

12 large eggs, hard boiled and peeled
2/3 cup mayonnaise, divided
1/8 teaspoon salt
1/4 teaspoon pepper
1/4 cup crumbled bleu cheese
1/4 cup chopped pecans, toasted
2 tablespoons finely chopped red onion
24 pecan halves, toasted

Slice the eggs in half lengthwise and carefully remove the yolks, leaving the egg white "shells" intact. Place the egg white shells in a single layer either on a serving plate or in an airtight container and set aside.

Combine the yolks with half of the mayonnaise in a bowl; mash with a fork until smooth. Add the salt, pepper and remaining mayonnaise; stir until smooth. Add the bleu cheese and pecans; stir well.

Spoon the yolk mixture into the egg white shells and garnish each with a chopped red onion. Cover tightly and refrigerate until serving.

Be-Deviled Eggs

BLACK-EYED PEA DIP

ABOUT 5 CUPS

You can make this recipe a day ahead and serve the dip either cold or warm.

3 (15-oz) cans black-eyed peas, divided
1 (8-oz) package cream cheese, softened
2 tablespoons hot water
1/4 cup butter
1/2 cup chopped onion
1 clove garlic, minced
1/4 teaspoon pepper
1 (10-oz) can tomatoes with green chilies
1 cup shredded sharp cheddar cheese
2 tablespoons chopped parsley
1 diced tomato

Empty 2 of the cans of black-eyed-peas into a colander; rinse and let drain. Combine the rinsed, drained peas, cream cheese and hot water in a food processor; process until smooth. Scrape the mixture into a bowl and set aside.

Empty the remaining can of peas into a colander; rinse and let drain. Add the peas to the cream cheese mixture, stir well and set aside.

Melt the butter in a large skillet over medium high heat; add the onion and sauté 3 minutes or until very soft. Add the garlic and pepper; stir to mix and sauté 1 minute. Remove the pan from the heat. Stir the onion mixture into cream cheese mixture and spoon into a shallow dish. Spoon the tomatoes evenly over the top and sprinkle with the cheese and tomatoes.

To serve the dip warm, preheat the oven to 350° and bake, uncovered, for 20 minutes or until the cheese is bubbly and dip is hot. Remove the dish from the oven and place in a thermal carrying bag. Just before serving, sprinkle the chopped parsley over the top.

To serve the dip cold, cover tightly and refrigerate until serving time. Just before serving, sprinkle the chopped parsley over the top and serve with assorted scoop-shaped chips, crackers, pita bread triangles and bread sticks.

Black-Eyed Pea Dip

2ND QUARTER
s i d e   d i s h e s

E ven the best quarterback needs a strong offensive line. Look through this section and you'll find a wide range of side dishes to round out your game day feast. Get-Thee-Behind-Me Deviled Corn, Grilled Garlic Toast, End Zone Green Beans and other great sides will make sure you don't have a mile-long line at the grill. You can prepare most of them the night before to cut down on prep time until you ring the dinner bell. Whether you're looking for a new way to serve up potatoes, or want to throw in some roughage to complement the main course, you'll find it in this collection of side dishes.

Left: Creamy Corn Casserole, *page 43*
Right: Potato Wedges, *page 42*

BREAD RECIPES

STUFFED CHEESE BREAD

6-8 SERVINGS

1 large, unsliced loaf French or Italian bread
2 cups grated Jarlsberg or Gruyère cheese
1/2 cup grated Parmesan cheese
1/4-1/2 cup capers
1 medium-size onion, finely chopped
4 tablespoons butter or margarine, softened
1/2 jar marinated red pepper strips

Preheat oven to 350°.

Slice the bread in half lengthwise three-quarters of the way to the end of the loaf; scoop out the soft part and discard. Combine the remaining ingredients in a bowl and mix well. Spread the cheese mixture into the hollowed-out loaf. Arrange on top of the cheese mixture.

Wrap the filled loaf in foil, place on a baking pan and bake for 2-3 minutes on the grill. Remove from the grill and cut into 1 to 1 1/2-inch slices; serve warm.

CRANBERRY BREAD

1 LOAF OR 18 MUFFINS

2 cups all-purpose flour
1 cup sugar
1-1 1/2 teaspoons baking powder
1 teaspoon salt
1/2 teaspoon baking soda
1/4 cup butter or margarine
3/4 cup orange juice
1 tablespoon grated orange peel
1 egg
1-1 1/2 cups fresh or frozen cranberries
1/2 cup chopped walnuts

Preheat the oven to 350°. Grease and flour 8 x 4 x 2-inch loaf pan.

Combine the flour, sugar, baking powder, salt and baking soda in a bowl.

Combine the orange juice, orange peel, butter and egg in a large bowl, food processor or mixer; beat until smooth. Add the flour mixture and stir just until blended. Add the cranberries and walnuts; beat until just combined.

Spoon the batter into the prepared pan. Bake for 65-70 minutes for loaf, 30 minutes for muffins, or until a wooden pick inserted near the center comes out clean. Remove from the oven and let cool for 10 minutes; turn out onto a wire rack and let cool completely.

TAILGATING TIPS

* Be prepared. Do some of your prep work the night before. For instance, chop vegetables and store in separate resealable bags and containers to keep flavors from mingling and save time. Marinate pork, beef and chicken in resealable bags.

* Instead of loose ice, consider freezing water in a lightweight plastic milk jug and putting it in your cooler to keep everything cold-that way, you won't flood the cooler and will end up with a clean supply of cool drinking water post-game.

* Eat and eat some more! Cook extra food, share it with tailgate neighbors and swap recipes.

GRILLED GARLIC TOAST

1/2-lb butter, softened
1/2-lb margarine, softened
1 cup chopped parsley
1/2 cup Parmesan cheese (optional)
8-12 cloves garlic, minced
1 loaf Italian bread, cut into thick slices

Combine all of the ingredients except the bread in a bowl; mix well. Spread mixture on one side of each bread slice; place on a hot grill until toasted.

BUTTERMILK-SCALLION CORNBREAD

12 WEDGES OR SQUARES
3/4 cup flour
11/2 cups stone-ground (white or yellow) cornmeal
2 teaspoons baking powder
3/4 teaspoon salt
11/4 cups buttermilk
3 tablespoons butter, melted
2 tablespoons honey
2 eggs
1/2 cup thinly sliced scallions

Preheat the oven to 400°. Lightly coat a 9-inch round or square baking pan with cooking spray.

Lightly spoon the flour into measuring cups; level with a knife. Combine the flour, cornmeal, baking powder and salt in a large bowl.

Combine the buttermilk, melted butter, honey and eggs in a small bowl; whisk to mix well. Add the buttermilk mixture to the cornmeal mixture; stir just until combined. Add the sliced scallions and stir until mixed. Scrape the batter into the prepared pan. Bake for 15 minutes or until either the edges are lightly browned or a wooden pick inserted in the center comes out clean. Remove the pan from the oven; serve warm.

How bad did Auburn beat Bama in the Tigers' first visit to Bryant-Denny Stadium in 2000? The closest the Tide came to scoring was a missed 48-yard field goal with a little more than a minute to go in the game. For the record, Alabama rushed for just 23 yards and made only eight first downs. The Tide's total yardage? One hundred, thirty-five, just five yards less than Rudi Johnson ran for ALL BY HIMSELF. "They just lined up and whipped us," Alabama coach Mike DuBose said. Damn sure did. And you liked it.

SALAD RECIPES

BLACK-EYED PEA SALAD
1-lb fresh or frozen black-eyed peas, cooked, drained and chilled
2 cups chopped tomatoes
🌶 1 (16-oz) jar of Porky's Bellycheer Wow Chow (mild or hot)

Combine the chilled, cooked black-eyed peas with the tomatoes and Porky's Wow Chow in a serving bowl. Toss to mix. Cover and refrigerate until ready to serve.

RED CABBAGE COLESLAW
ABOUT 7 1/2 CUPS
You can make this recipe a day ahead and refrigerate it until serving time; the slaw will go from super crunchy to a more tender texture the longer it stands.
4 cups thinly sliced red cabbage
4 cups shredded carrots
1/4 cup chopped red onion
1/4 cup chopped fresh parsley
3 tablespoons red wine vinegar
3 tablespoons extra-virgin olive oil
1 tablespoon honey
1 tablespoon whole-grain prepared mustard
1/2 teaspoon salt
1/4 teaspoon pepper

Combine the cabbage, carrot, onion and parsley in a large bowl; stir to mix.

Combine the remaining ingredients in a small bowl; stir with a whisk until well mixed. Drizzle the dressing over the cabbage mixture and toss to combine. Adjust salt and pepper to taste; cover and refrigerate until serving time.

PORKY'S BARBECUE SLAW
4 cups shredded cabbage
1/3 cup sugar
1/2 cup vinegar
🌶 1 cup Porky's Historic Lynchburg Jalapeño Ketchup
1 teaspoon salt
1/2 teaspoon pepper

Combine all of the ingredients in a large bowl; mix well. Cover tightly and refrigerate until serving time.

Connie Frederick couldn't resist. Auburn was whipping Bama by more than three touchdowns with less than a minute to go in the 1969 game. Frederick was lined up to punt deep in his own territory. But he knew full well he wasn't going to punt. Not on this day. Auburn hadn't beaten Alabama since 1963 and Frederick let out six years' worth of frustration by tucking the ball and rambling 84 yards for one, last take-that-Bama TD. The final score was 49-26 and those 49 Auburn points were the most scored against Alabama since 1907. And Frederick's touchdown run was, at the time, the second-longest in AU history. Frederick's fake punt was a surprise even to his teammates. "I didn't tell the team," he said. "I didn't tell anybody. I just grabbed the ball and hauled."

2ND QUARTER
side dishes

SAMMY THE GREEK'S PICNIC SALAD

4 SERVINGS

1 (14 1/2-oz) can vegetable broth

1 1/2 cups couscous

1 small red bell pepper, coarsely diced

1 small yellow bell pepper, coarsely diced

1 (14-oz) can artichoke hearts, drained and quartered

1 (14-oz) can chickpeas (garbanzo beans), drained

1 cup sliced green onions

8-oz feta cheese, crumbled

1/2 cup sliced black olives

1/4-1/2 cup favorite vinaigrette

1 small head romaine lettuce, separated into leaves

Pour the broth into a saucepan and bring to a boil; stir in the couscous, remove from heat, cover and let stand for 5 minutes. Spoon the couscous into a large mixing bowl and fluff with a fork; let stand for 5 minutes and then fluff again.

Add the bell peppers, artichokes, chickpeas, green onions, cheese, olives and celery; stir gently to mix. Pour the vinaigrette over the couscous mixture and toss gently. To serve, make a bed of lettuce leaves on a shallow serving dish and spoon the couscous mixture on top.

"I didn't know what to think. It scared me to death. Both of the balls looked identical to me. They just bounced into my hands. All I had to do was pick it up and run. It was by far the greatest thrill I've ever had."

–David Langner, after running back not one, but two, blocked punts to beat Bama 17-16 in 1972.

PASTA SALAD

12 CUPS

1 (16-oz) package penne pasta, cooked, rinsed, drained and cooled

1 green bell pepper, diced

1/2-lb salami or pepperoni, chopped

5 whole pepperoncini, finely chopped

1/3 cup extra-virgin olive oil

2 cloves garlic, minced

1/4 cup finely grated Parmesan cheese

1/4 cup white wine vinegar

1/4 cup chopped fresh parsley

1/4 cup chopped fresh basil

1 teaspoon salt

1/4 teaspoon pepper

Coarsely ground black pepper

Combine the cooled pasta, green pepper, salami and pepperoncini in a large bowl; stir to mix. In a separate bowl combine the olive oil, garlic, cheese, vinegar, parsley, basil, salt and pepper; stir with a whisk until well combined. Drizzle the dressing over the pasta mixture; toss to coat. Cover and refrigerate; serve with coarsely ground black pepper.

C O R N B R E A D   S A L A D

6 SERVINGS

2 (8-oz) boxes cornbread mix
1 can whole kernel corn
2 cups Miracle Whip
4 green onions, chopped
1 chopped bell pepper
3 tomatoes, chopped
4 boiled eggs, chopped
10-oz grated cheese

Bake cornbread according to package directions. Crumble cornbread in a large bowl. Combine corn and mayonnaise with crumbled cornbread. Add bell pepper, eggs, green onions, tomatoes, and cheese. Stir to mix. Chill for 12 hours before serving.

H E A R T Y   G R E E N   S A L A D   W I T H   M A N D A R I N   O R A N G E S   A N D   G O A T   C H E E S E

ABOUT 8 CUPS

Travel tips: Use hearty greens that resist wilting. Pack the salad ingredients, dressing, cheese and toppings separately. Pack the dressing in a jar with a tightly fitting lid. Just before serving, give the jar a quick shake to remix the dressing, drizzle it over the salad and toss or serve the dressing on the side.

Hearty Green Salad and
Take-Out Fried Chicken

4 cups escarole, torn into bite-size pieces
4 cups romaine, torn into bite-size pieces
1 cup mandarin orange segments in light syrup, drained (reserve syrup) or 1 cup sliced fresh apple or pear tossed with lemon juice, drained (reserve lemon juice)
1 cup thinly sliced (vertically) red onion
1/4 cup white balsamic vinegar
2 tablespoons reserved light syrup from mandarin oranges or reserved lemon juice
3 tablespoons extra-virgin olive oil
1/4 teaspoon salt
1/4 teaspoon pepper
1 (4-oz) package goat cheese or bleu cheese, crumbled
Optional toppings: chopped walnuts, toasted slivered almonds
fried Chinese noodles,croutons, coarsely ground black pepper, kosher salt

Combine the escarole, romaine, mandarin oranges (or chopped apple or pear) and red onion slices in a large bowl; toss gently to combine. Combine the balsamic vinegar, reserved light syrup (or reserved lemon juice), olive oil, salt and pepper in a small bowl; whisk to mix well. Drizzle the dressing over the salad and toss gently to combine; sprinkle with the cheese and any of the optional toppings, as desired.

RED-JACKET POTATO SALAD

YIELD: ABOUT 12 CUPS

You can create your own variation of this cold potato salad by adding your favorite herbs and spices such as dill and mustard seeds, chives and fresh horseradish. You can make it a day ahead and refrigerate until serving time.

1 cup sour cream

1/2 cup mayonnaise

3 tablespoons white wine vinegar or white vinegar

1/4 teaspoon salt

1/4 teaspoon pepper

1/2 cup sliced green onions

4-lbs small (unpeeled) red potatoes, cooked and cut into bite-size chunks

1 tablespoon chopped parsley

1/2 teaspoon caraway seeds

Combine the sour cream, mayonnaise, vinegar, salt and pepper in a large bowl; blend well. Add the potatoes and toss gently to mix. Cover and refrigerate until serving time. Just before serving, sprinkle the parsley and caraway seeds over the top.

ONE-DISH LAYERED SALAD

Make this salad the night before your tailgate party.

1 head lettuce, torn into bite-size pieces, or 1 package mixed salad greens, torn into bite-size pieces

1 small package frozen tiny baby or English peas, uncooked

3-4 green onions, thinly sliced

4 hard boiled eggs, sliced

2 cups mayonnaise or sandwich spread

2 tablespoons sugar

2 tablespoons wine vinegar

8-oz shredded cheese

10 strips bacon, cooked and crumbled

Layer in order, the lettuce, peas, green onions and egg slices in a large serving bowl. Combine the mayonnaise, sugar and wine vinegar. Mix well and spread over the top of the layered ingredients. Sprinkle the cheese and crumbled bacon on top. Seal the bowl with plastic wrap and refrigerate overnight.

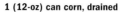

BLACK BEAN-AND-SALSA SALAD

You can make the corn-black bean mixture and the salsa-dressing mixture ahead of time. Carry the two mixtures and the salad greens to the stadium separately and toss them together just before serving.

1 (12-oz) can corn, drained
1 (15-oz) black beans, drained and rinsed
1 1/2 cups chopped celery
1/2 cup chopped green onions
1/4 cup chopped cilantro
1 (14-oz) jar salsa
1/4 cup wine vinegar dressing
Salad greens

Combine the corn, black beans, celery, onions and cilantro in a bowl; mix well. Combine the salsa and dressing in another bowl; mix well. When ready to serve, place the salad greens in a large serving bowl. Add the corn-black bean mixture and the salsa-dressing mixture; toss to mix.

GREEK BEEF SALAD

6-8 SERVINGS

2-lbs cooked roast beef, slivered
1 green bell pepper, cut into strips
1 red bell pepper, cut into strips
1 red onion, sliced
2 cups sliced ripe olives
1 cup sliced green olives
8-oz feta cheese, crumbled
1 (6-oz) jar marinated artichoke hearts, drained (reserve liquid) and diced
1 cup minced fresh parsley
Olive oil
1/3 cup red wine vinegar
2 cloves garlic, minced
1 teaspoon basil
1 teaspoon oregano
1/2 teaspoon tarragon
Salt, to taste
Pepper, to taste

Combine the beef, peppers, onion, olives, cheese, artichokes and parsley in a large bowl. Add enough olive oil to the reserved artichoke liquid to make 2/3 cup and combine with the vinegar, garlic, basil, oregano, tarragon, salt and pepper in a small bowl; whisk until well mixed. Pour the dressing over the beef mixture. Cover tightly and refrigerate overnight. Serve chilled.

RICE SALAD
8-10 SERVINGS
1 cup chopped green pepper
1/2 cup green onions, chopped
1/2 cup olive oil
1/4 cup cider vinegar
1/2 teaspoon salt
1 cup long-grain rice, cooked
1 cup sliced fresh mushrooms
1/4 cup chopped dates
3/4 cup raisins
1/2 cup slivered almonds
Lettuce

Combine the green pepper, green onions, cooked rice in a large bowl; mix well. Gently fold in the mushrooms, raisins, dates and nuts.

Mix the olive oil, cider vinegar and salt in a small bowl. Pour 1/2 of vinegarette over the rice mixture; toss to coat. Cover and refrigerate overnight. Store remaining vinegarette in the refrigerator. Just before serving, add remaining vinegarette and stir to mix well. Serve chilled in a lettuce-lined bowl.

"This is why they built this pretty stadium. This is why we got the game here. This is what it's all about."

–Auburn senior linebacker Quentin Riggins after Auburn scored 23 second-half points to cruise past Alabama 30-20 in the first-ever game between the two teams on Auburn's home field.

BEAN RECIPES

BEEF 'N' BEAN BARBECUE
1-lb ground beef
1 (8-oz) can tomato sauce
1 can (2 1/2 cups) pork and beans
1/2 cup water
1/2 cup chopped onion
1/2 cup chopped celery
1/4 cup chopped green pepper
1 clove garlic
2 tablespoons vinegar
1 tablespoon brown sugar
1 teaspoon dry mustard
1/2 teaspoon thyme

Preheat the oven to 375°.

Place the ground beef in a skillet, and cook over medium heat until browned. Add the onion, celery, and green pepper; cook until the vegetables are soft. Stir in the tomato sauce, water, garlic, brown sugar, mustard, thyme, and vinegar, and simmer for 3-4 minutes; add the pork and beans. Remove from the heat, and pour into a casserole dish; bake at 375° for 45 minutes.

MARDIS W. HOWLE, JR'S COSTA RICAN BLACK BEANS

SERVES 8-10

6-oz thick smoked bacon, finely diced
1 cup diced yellow onion
4 cloves garlic, finely chopped
2 jalapeño chilies, finely chopped
8-oz sausage, diced
1/2 cup ketchup
1/2 cup yellow mustard
1 teaspoon Colman's mustard powder
1/2 teaspoon ground ginger
1/2 cup dark rum
2 tablespoons brown sugar
1/2 cup light molasses
1 tablespoon hot sauce
2 tablespoons Worcestershire sauce
3 (15-oz) cans black beans, drained
Salt

Grill bacon in a large saucepan over medium heat until crispy. Without removing the bacon, add the onion, garlic and jalapeños. Reduce heat and sauté for five minutes, until the onions are tender and clear.

Add all other ingredients EXCEPT for the black beans. Increase heat and bring the mixture to a boil, then reduce heat and let simmer.

Drain the beans and rinse with cool water using a colander. Add to the sauce and stir well. Simmer over low heat for about an hour and season with salt. Serve hot, or reheat when you're ready to eat.

BAKED LIMA BEANS

6 SERVINGS

You can make this recipe ahead of time, and serve it either hot or cold.

2 cups dried lima beans
2 tablespoons butter
1 small onion, chopped
1 green bell pepper, chopped
2 cups cooked tomatoes, strained
1/2 teaspoon salt
1/8 teaspoon cayenne pepper
1 teaspoon Worcestershire sauce
1 cup grated Pepper Jack cheese

Prepare the lima beans according to the package directions.

Preheat the oven to 350°. Grease a casserole dish. Melt the butter in a skillet over medium heat; add the onion and bell pepper, and sauté until the onion is tender. Add the tomatoes, and simmer 10 minutes. Add the prepared beans, salt, cayenne pepper, and Worcestershire sauce; mix well.

Spoon alternate layers of the bean mixture and cheese into the casserole; bake at 350° for 20-30 minutes. Serve immediately, or store in the refrigerator.

MAPLE-BACON BAKED BEANS

6 CUPS

You can make this recipe a day ahead and serve the beans either hot or at room temperature.

8 slices bacon

1/4 cup maple syrup

3 tablespoons prepared brown mustard

1 tablespoon barbecue sauce

1/4 teaspoon salt

1/4 teaspoon pepper

2 (15.75-oz) cans pork and beans

1 (15-oz) can kidney beans, drained

1 (16-oz) can butter beans, drained

Preheat the oven to 350°.

Cook the bacon in a large skillet over medium high heat until crisp. Remove the pan from the heat. Place the bacon on layers of paper towels. When cool and well drained, crumble and set aside. Reserve 1 tablespoon of the drippings and discard the rest.

Maple-Bacon Baked Beans, Red-Jacket Potato Salad *page 37* and Take-Out Fried Chicken

Combine the reserved bacon drippings, maple syrup, mustard, barbecue sauce, salt and pepper in a bowl. Add the pork and beans, kidney beans and butter beans; stir gently to combine. Stir in half of the crumbled bacon.

Spoon the bean mixture into a 2-quart baking dish and bake for 30 minutes, or until bubbly, stirring occasionally. Remove the pan from the oven and sprinkle the remaining crumbled bacon over the top. Serve hot, or cover and refrigerate overnight. Either reheat before serving or let the beans warm to room temperature.

PEPPER JACK LIMA BEANS

6 SERVINGS

You can make this recipe ahead of time and serve it either hot or cold.

2 cups dried lima beans
2 tablespoons butter
1 small onion, chopped
2 cups cooked tomatoes with chilis, strained
1/2 teaspoon salt
1/8 teaspoon cayenne pepper
1 teaspoon Worcestershire sauce
1 cup grated pepper jack cheese

Prepare the lima beans according to the package directions.

Preheat oven to 350°. Grease a casserole dish.

Melt the butter in a skillet over medium heat. Add the onion and bell pepper and sauté until the onion is tender. Add the tomatoes and simmer 10 minutes. Add the prepared beans, salt, cayenne pepper and Worcestershire sauce; mix well.

Spoon alternate layers of the bean mixture and cheese into the prepared dish; bake for 20-30 minutes.

VEGETABLE RECIPES

POTATO WEDGES

12 SERVINGS

2 tablespoons butter
1 clove garlic, minced
1 1/2 teaspoon flour
3/4 cup milk
1/8 teaspoon dry mustard
1/2 cup shredded sharp cheddar cheese
3 hot baked potatoes, each cut into 4 wedges
Optional toppings: crumbled bacon, minced chives, chopped parsley, sour cream, coarsely ground black pepper

Preheat oven to 450°. Place potato wedges on a large baking sheet; coat well with cooking spray. Bake for 25 minutes or until browned and tender, turning occasionally. Remove from the oven and sprinkle with salt to taste.

Spoon the cheese sauce over the hot potato wedges and top with desired toppings.

CREAMY CORN CASEROLE

10 SERVINGS

Preparation tip: *Prepare the corn mixture ahead of time and reheat it in the microwave. Prepare the breadcrumbs and then broil as directed below.*

3/4 cup half and half

4 tablespoons butter, melted and divided

1 tablespoon flour

3/4 teaspoon salt

1/4 teaspoon pepper

2 tablespoons diced pimiento

Dash nutmeg

1 (15-oz) can creamed corn

1 (16-oz) package frozen corn kernels, thawed

3 egg yolks, beaten

1 cup fresh breadcrumbs

Lightly coat a 2 quart casserole dish with cooking spray.

Combine the half and half, 2 tablespoons of the melted butter, flour, salt, pepper, and nutmeg in a saucepan. Place the pan over medium high heat, and bring the mixture to a boil, stirring constantly. Cook for 1 minute or until thickened, stirring constantly. Add the creamed corn, and stir to mix; cook 1 minute. Add the corn kernels and egg yolks; cook 3 minutes or until hot and thickened, stirring constantly. Remove the pan from the heat, stir in pimiento and spoon the mixture into the prepared casserole dish.

Preheat the broiler. Combine the remaining 2 tablespoons of melted butter and the breadcrumbs in a small bowl; toss with a fork. Sprinkle the breadcrumbs evenly over the corn mixture, and broil for 2 minutes or until golden brown.

AUBURN ORANGE CANDIED YAMS

6 SERVINGS

1/4 cup water
2 tablespoons frozen orange juice concentrate
1 cup brown sugar
1/2 teaspoon cinnamon
6 medium-size yams or sweet potatoes, boiled and peeled
1/2 cup butter, melted

Preheat the oven to 350°. Grease an 11 x 13-inch baking dish.

Pour the water into a saucepan. Add the brown sugar and orange juice concentrate. Cook over low heat until the sugar dissolves; remove from the heat.

Cut the yams lengthwise and arrange in the bottom of the prepared dish. Spoon the melted butter over the yams and top with the melted sugar mixture. Bake for 35–45 minutes.

GET-THEE-BEHIND-ME DEVILED CORN

8-10 SERVINGS

4 tablespoons butter
2 tablespoons flour
1/2 cup milk
1 tablespoon lemon juice
1 teaspoon Dijon mustard
1/2 teaspoon Worcestershire sauce
1/2 teaspoon salt
1/2 teaspoon pepper
3 slices bacon, cooked and crumbled
1 (16-oz) can yellow corn, drained
1 (16-oz) can cream-style yellow corn
1/2 cup parmesan cheese
1 tablespoon butter, melted
1/2 cup seasoned breadcrumbs
3 hard boiled eggs, cut into wedges
8 green olives, sliced

Preheat the oven to 350°. Grease a 1 1/2-quart casserole dish.

Melt 4 tablespoons of the butter in a large saucepan; stir in the flour, milk, lemon juice, mustard, Worcestershire sauce, salt and pepper. Cook over medium heat for 8 minutes or until the mixture thickens, stirring frequently. Remove from the heat and stir in the bacon, corn and cream-style corn. Pour the corn mixture into prepared dish; sprinkle with the cheese.

Combine the melted butter and breadcrumbs in a small bowl; mix well and sprinkle over the casserole. Bake for 45 minutes; remove from the oven. Just before serving, garnish with the egg wedges and olive slices.

RATATOUILLE

6-8 SERVINGS

Make this recipe at least one day ahead of time; you can store it in the refrigerator for up to 4 days.

2 (1-lb) eggplants, peeled (if desired)

1/4 cup olive or salad oil

2 medium-size onions, coarsely chopped

2 large green peppers, seeded and coarsely chopped

3 large zucchini, cut into 1/2-inch slices

4 large tomatoes, peeled and coarsely chopped

4 cloves garlic, minced or pressed

1 teaspoon salt

1 teaspoon basil

1 teaspoon thyme

1/2 teaspoon oregano

1/4 teaspoon pepper

2 bay leaves

Cut the eggplants crosswise into 1/2-inch slices; cut each slice into four pieces. Place in a colander, rinse, sprinkle with salt and set aside to drain for 30 minutes. Heat the oil in a large cooking pot over medium high heat; add the onions and green peppers and cook, stirring, until the onions are soft. Add the eggplant and zucchini and cook, stirring often, until lightly browned.

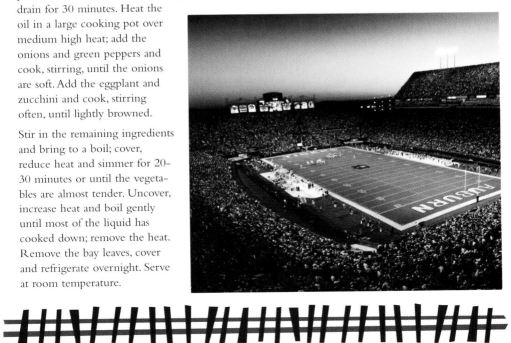

Stir in the remaining ingredients and bring to a boil; cover, reduce heat and simmer for 20-30 minutes or until the vegetables are almost tender. Uncover, increase heat and boil gently until most of the liquid has cooked down; remove the heat. Remove the bay leaves, cover and refrigerate overnight. Serve at room temperature.

MATCHSTICK CARROTS

2-lb carrots, peeled and cut into matchstick-size pieces
1 green pepper, chopped
1 medium onion, thinly sliced
1/4 cup vegetable oil
1/3 cup vinegar
1/2 cup granulated sugar
1 (10 1/2-oz) can condensed tomato soup
1 tablespoon Worcestershire sauce
1/2 teaspoon salt
1 teaspoon dry mustard

Cook carrots in boiling water for 2-3 minutes. Do not overcook. The carrots should remain crunchy.

While carrots are cooking, combine the other ingredients and mix well. Add carrots to sauce and mix gently so as not to break carrots. Allow to sit overnight for flavors to blend.

FIELD GOAL GREEN BEANS

8-10 fresh basil leaves, chopped
2 tablespoons chopped fresh parsley
1 tablespoon fresh oregano
5 tablespoons balsamic vinegar
2 tablespoons chopped onion
2 cloves garlic, minced
1-lb fresh green beans, rinsed and snapped
1/3 cup olive oil
Salt, to taste
Pepper, to taste

Combine the basil, parsley, oregano and vinegar in a large bowl; mix well and let stand for 10 minutes. Stir in the onion and garlic.

Drop the green beans into boiling water and cook until the beans start to get tender; drain well. Immediately add the cooked beans to the basil mixture and stir to mix; let stand for 1 hour. Add the olive oil, salt and pepper just before serving; serve at room temperature.

MARINATED GREEN BEANS

4 SERVINGS

1/4 cup olive oil

1 onion, finely chopped

2 tomatoes, peeled and diced

1-lb fresh green beans, cut into 1-inch pieces

1/2 cup water

1 teaspoon sugar

1 teaspoon salt

Heat the oil in a large skillet; add the onion and sauté until the onion is transparent. Add the remaining ingredients and cook until the beans are tender. Remove from the heat, spoon into a serving bowl, cover and refrigerate until serving time. Serve cold.

HASH POTATO CASSEROLE

12-16 SERVINGS

2 (10 3/4-oz) cans condensed cream of chicken soup

1 cup sour cream

1/2 teaspoon garlic salt

1 (2-lb) package frozen cubed hash brown potatoes

1 cup diced ham

2 cups Colby cheese, grated

1/2 cup grated Parmesan cheese

Preheat the oven to 350°. Grease a 13 x 9-inch baking dish.

Combine the soup, sour cream and garlic salt in a large bowl; stir to mix. Add the potatoes, ham and cheddar cheese; stir to mix well. Pour the mixture into the prepared dish; top with the Parmesan cheese. Bake, uncovered, for 55-60 minutes or until the potatoes are tender.

SUFFERING SUCCOTASH

6-8 SERVINGS

2-lb fresh green beans, cut into 1-inch pieces

1/4 lb salt pork, thinly sliced

1 (16-oz) can cream-style corn

2 tablespoons butter

1/4 cup sugar

Place the green beans into a large saucepan; cover with water, bring to a boil and cook until the beans are tender. Brown the salt pork in a small skillet over medium heat; remove from the heat and add the pork to the beans. Add the corn, butter and sugar. Simmer over low heat for 1 hour, stirring frequently.

Second Down Menu

Be-Deviled Eggs(p28)

✕

Black-Eyed Pea Dip served with chips and pita bread triangles(p29)

✕

Your Favorite Take-Out Fried Chicken

✕

Maple-Bacon Baked Beans(p41)

✕

Red-Jacket Potato Salad(p37)

✕

Super Shortbread Cookies(p85)

✕

Almond Bars(p87)

✕

Chocolate-Chunk Red Velvet Sheet Cake (p76)

3RD QUARTER
m a i n   d i s h e s

Well, we can't blame you for starting here. This is the center of any tail-gating party – the main course, meat and fire. Whether you're cooking slab after slab of ribs for an army or a pack of hot dogs for the kids, this section has all the tips to spice it up. From Chili Dogs to a Marinated Beef Fillet, from Brunswick Stew to Bourbon-Glazed Ham, you'll find recipes to cook all your main courses to perfection. Simmered, grilled, smoked or roasted; it's all on the menu.

Left: Jalapeño topped Barkley's Best Chili, *page 61*, and Buttermilk-Scallion Cornbread, *page 33*

Right: Spicy Grilled Shrimp Skewers, *page 52*; Pasta Salad, *page 35*; and Red Cabbage Slaw, *page 34*

PORKY'S BELLYCHEER HOT AND SPICY SHRIMP

2-lbs large or jumbo shrimp (peeled and deveined)
4 tablespoons Belllycheer Jalapeño Pepper Sauce
1/2 stick melted butter or margarine
1 tablespoon Bellycheer Blazin' Cajun SeasonZing
11/2 teaspoons Bellycheer Seafood SeasonZing
Juice from 1 Lemon

Combine butter, Bellycheer Jalapeño Pepper Sauce, Blazin' Cajun SeasonZing and Seafood SeasonZing. Marinate shrimp for 2 hours, without lemon juice. Drain and reserve liquid.

Place shrimp on skewers and grill for approximately 3 1/2 minutes per side, or until done.

Add lemon juice to reserved marinade for basting while grilling. In lieu of grilling you can stir fry in a small amount of oil and marinade.

BLAZIN' CAJUN FRIED CATFISH

SERVES 4

8 catfish fillets
5 teaspoons Bellycheer Blazin' Cajun SeasonZing
1 tablespoon Bellycheer Jalapeño Hot Sauce
11/2 cups self-rising cornmeal
1/2 cup self-rising flour
1 teaspoon salt
1 teaspoon black pepper
2 cups peanut or canola oil

Wash the catfish fillets and pat dry. In a bowl combine catfish and Jalapeño Pepper Sauce, thinly coating each fillet. Then sprinkle each side of the fillets with 1/2 tsp. Blazin' Cajun Seasoning and gently rub in. Combine cornmeal, flour, salt, black pepper and 1tsp. Blazin' Cajun Seasoning in a brown paper sack and shake to blend well. Heat oil in large skillet. Add fillets 1 or 2 at a time to bag and shake to coat fish. Then immediately transfer fish to the hot oil and cook, turning often until golden brown–about 6 to 8 minutes. Drain on paper towels and serve immediately with slaw, french fries and hushpuppies.

SAUCY SHISH KABOBS

1 cup olive oil
3/4 cup soy sauce
1 (6-oz) can orange juice
1/4 cup Worcestershire sauce
1/4 cup prepared mustard
1/2 teaspoon garlic powder
1/2 teaspoon ground ginger
Meat of choice, cut into large cubes
Vegetables of choice, cut into large cubes
Lemons, cut into quarters

Combine all of the ingredients except the meat, vegetables and lemons in a blender or mixing bowl; blend until well mixed. Place the meat cubes into a shallow bowl or heavy-duty, self-sealing plastic bag; reserve 1/2 cup of the olive oil mixture and pour the rest over the meat. Cover the bowl or seal the bag, place in the refrigerator and marinate overnight.

Remove the meat from the dish or bag and discard the marinade. Squeeze the lemons over the meat. Arrange lemon quarters, the meat cubes and vegetables on skewers and place on a hot grill. Cook over low or medium heat until desired doneness, basting frequently with the reserved olive oil mixture.

RIB-EYE CUBANO

4 SERVINGS
4 (6-oz) rib-eye steaks
3 fresh limes
4 cloves garlic, chopped
1 tablespoon ground red chili pepper
1 teaspoon freshly ground black pepper
1 teaspoon ground cumin
1/4 cup olive oil
1/4 cup cilantro
Coarse sea salt, to taste
8 lime wedges

Place the steaks in a shallow dish. Cut the limes in half and squeeze the juice over both sides of the steaks. Rub the steaks with the garlic and sprinkle with the chili pepper, black pepper and cumin; cover the dish tightly and refrigerate for at least 30 minutes.

When ready to grill, brush the steaks with the oil and grill for 7 minutes on each side (for medium doneness). Remove from the grill and cut the steaks into 1/4-inch cubes. Just before serving, add the cilantro and sprinkle with coarse sea salt. Serve with lime wedges for garnish.

"The saddest thing about it is, Alabama won't be remembered as a great championship team. They had a great season. Unfortunately, they had to come here to play us."

–Auburn running back
James Joseph, after Auburn
defeated previously unbeaten
Alabama 30-20 in 1989.

SPICY GRILLED SHRIMP SKEWERS

Preparation and grilling tips: *Make the marinade a day ahead; 30 minutes before grilling, thread the shrimp on skewers, place in a deep pan, pour the marinade over the skewered shrimp and refrigerate. For large quantities of shrimp, grill in a basket instead of on skewers.*

2 (8-oz) cans tomato sauce with Italian herbs

1/2 cup olive oil

2 tablespoons red wine vinegar

1/2 teaspoon black pepper

1/2 teaspoon cayenne pepper

8 cloves garlic, minced

3-lbs peeled, deveined shrimp

Bamboo or metal skewers

Bottled hot sauce

Combine the tomato sauce, olive oil, vinegar, black pepper, cayenne pepper and garlic in a bowl; stir with a whisk until combined. Add the shrimp, stirring to coat. Cover and refrigerate for only 30 minutes (marinating more than 30 minutes can affect the texture of the shrimp).

While the shrimp is marinating, prepare the grill. Thread the shrimp onto bamboo or metal skewers; grill 3 minutes per side or until shrimp are done. Serve with the hot sauce on the side.

BASQUE KEBABS

SERVES 4.

1 1/2-lb boneless leg of lamb, cut into 1 1/2-inch cubes

1/2 cup olive oil

1/2 cup port wine

1/4 cup dried, minced onions

2 tablespoons cider vinegar

1 tablespoon cumin

8 10-inch skewers

Mix the oil and non-lamb ingredients together in a bowl. Set aside for a few minutes.

Put the lamb cubes in a large, non-aluminum bowl, then pour the mixture over the meat. Cover and let stand in the refrigerator for 2 to 4 hours.

Thread lamb cubes onto skewers. Grill the skewers over a medium-hot fire for about 12 minutes for medium rare, 15 minutes for medium well.

PORKY'S HICKORY SMOKED BABY BACK RIBS

1 (2¹/2 lb) slab pork baby back or St. Louis style ribs

🍖 2 level teaspoons Porky's Tennessee Master Que BBQ Seasoning & Rub

🍖 1 Bottle Porky's Tennessee Master Que BBQ Sauce

1 tablespoon brown sugar

Peel membrane from bone side of ribs. Sprinkle on 1 level teaspoon Tennessee Master Que BBQ Seasoning to each side of ribs. Wrap in plastic or foil and let marinate in refrigerator 2 hours to overnight.

Preheat smoker to approximately. 220°–225°. Add hickory chips to smoker and place ribs on rack bone side down. Smoke ribs for approximately 1¹/2 hours, then turn ribs over and smoke for additional 30 minutes.

Remove ribs from rack and place on a piece of heavy aluminum foil. Baste each side of ribs with approximately 1 tablespoon of Tennessee Master Que BBQ Sauce. Place the ribs bone side down and sprinkle with brown sugar.

Wrap foil around ribs. Place back on a smoker or in the oven at 225° for an additional 2¹/2 to 3 hours or until done. Remove from foil and baste with Tennessee Master Que BBQ Sauce just before serving. Serve with additional sauce on side.

LOVE ME BEEF TENDER

6-8 SERVINGS

1 (4¹/2-lb) beef tenderloin, trimmed

2 tablespoons sea salt

1 tablespoon freshly ground black pepper

3 tablespoons olive oil

1 tablespoon chopped garlic

1 tablespoon dry mustard

1 tablespoon Worcestershire sauce

Juice of 1 lemon

Rub the tenderloin with the salt and pepper and place in a shallow dish. Combine the oil, garlic, mustard, Worcestershire sauce and lemon juice in a small bowl; whisk until well blended and pour over the tenderloin, turning several times to coat. Cover the dish tightly and refrigerate for 1-2 hours.

Remove the meat from the marinade and place on the grill; discard the marinade. Cook the meat for 10 minutes on each side; remove it from the grill, wrap it in foil and return it to the grill. Cook for an additional 10-15 minutes or until desired doneness. Remove the meat from the grill and let it stand for 10 minutes before slicing and serving.

BELLYCHEER BURGER

4-lb. ground beef
1 medium onion, finely chopped
1 teaspoon freshly ground black pepper
1 teaspoon salt
2 tablespoons Bellycheer Jalapeño Hot Sauce
1 tablespoon Bellycheer Worcestershire Fire Sauce
1/2 teaspoon garlic powder
Bellycheer Steak & Burger SeaonZing

Mix all ingredients well. Shape into patties and cook on grill, broil or pan fry. Just before removing patties, sprinkle generously with Bellycheer Steak & Burger SeasonZing.

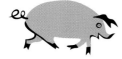

TOP CHOPS

SERVES 4
4 thick, center-cut pork chops
1/2 cup port wine
2 tablespoons dry mustard
1 tablespoon prepared horseradish
2 tablespoons orange juice
2 tablespoons soy sauce
1 teaspoon ground black pepper

Mix together all the non-pork ingredients in a bowl. Brush over chops just before grilling.

Grill the chops to your liking. Baste at will. Remove from heat and serve. These should be jumping right off the grill with flavor – no need to season at the table.

BLAZIN' CAJUN FRIED CHICKEN FILLETS

SERVES 4
8 boneless chicken fillets
5 tablespoons Bellycheer Blazin' Cajun SeasonZing
1 tablespoon Bellycheer Jalapeño Hot Sauce
1 1/2 cups self-rising cornmeal
1/2 cup self-rising flour
1 tablespoon salt
1 tablespoon black pepper
2 cups peanut or canola oil

Wash the chicken and pat dry. In a bowl combine chicken and Jalapeño Pepper Sauce, thinly coating each fillet. Then sprinkle each side of the fillets with 1/4 teaspoon Blazin' Cajun Seasoning and gently rub in. Combine cornmeal, flour, salt, black pepper and 1teaspoon Blazin' Cajun Seasoning in a brown paper sack and shake to blend well. Heat oil in large skillet. Add fillets 1 or 2 at a time to bag and shake to coat chicken. Then immediately transfer chicken to the hot oil and cook, turning often until golden brown–about 6 to 8 minutes. Drain on paper towels and serve immediately with slaw, french fries and hushpuppies.

BLEU BURGERS

15-20 SMALL BURGERS

You can make the burgers ahead of time and store them in the freezer. Allow them to thaw completely in the refrigerator before grilling.

2-lbs lean ground beef

1/2-lb bleu cheese, crumbled

4 green onions, thinly sliced

1 teaspoon salt

1 teaspoon pepper

1 teaspoon garlic powder

1 teaspoon crushed red pepper flakes

2 tablespoons Worcestershire sauce

1 tablespoon Tabasco sauce

1 egg, beaten

Potato rolls

Combine all of the ingredients except the rolls in a large bowl; mix thoroughly and shape into 15-20 burgers. Cook the burgers on a hot grill, turning only once. Serve on the potato rolls with your favorite condiments.

BOURBON-GLAZED HAM

Bake the ham a day or two ahead of time and store it in the refrigerator. Slice the ham thin and serve it with a variety of breads and rolls with your favorite condiments.

1/2-1 cup bourbon

1/2-1 cup dry red wine

1 cup brown sugar

6 bruised cloves

2 tablespoons grated orange peel

Fully cooked smoked ham, skinned

Combine all of the ingredients except the ham in a medium bowl and mix well; spread the mixture on the ham. Bake the ham as directed on the package, basting during the last half-hour of cooking.

TUNA STEAKS WITH CHILI SAUCE

SERVES 6

1/2 cup mayonnaise
2 tablespoons finely chopped chilies in adobo sauce
Salt and freshly ground black pepper
6 (6-oz) fillets sushi-grade tuna
2 tablespoons oil
Salt and freshly ground black pepper

Combine the mayonnaise and chilies and mix together in a small bowl. Add salt and pepper to taste and set aside.

Brush the fillets with oil and season with salt and pepper. Grill the fillets for 4 to 5 minutes, until lightly browned on the outside and firm and white on the inside. Using tongs or a spatula, carefully turn the fillets and continue to grill for another 3 to 4 minutes.

Serve hot. Either brush the mayonnaise on the tuna directly, or serve on the side.

JAMAICAN JERK CHICKEN

12 SERVINGS

3 red onions, chopped
3 cups chopped green bell pepper
3 cups extra virgin olive oil
1 1/2 cups white vinegar
1 1/2 cups soy sauce
1/3 cup ginger powder
1/3 cup Caribbean Jerk Seasoning
2 tablespoons cayenne pepper
1 tablespoon cinnamon
1 tablespoon allspice
1 tablespoon nutmeg
12 boneless chicken breasts, skinned

Combine all of the ingredients except the chicken in a food processor. Process until well blended. Pour the mixture into a shallow dish or a large heavy-duty, self-sealing plastic bag; add the chicken pieces and refrigerate overnight.

Remove the chicken and place the chicken on a hot grill; discard the marinade. When the chicken is almost cooked, remove it from the grill and cut it into strips; place the chicken strips back on the grill and cook an additional 5 minutes.

MARINATED FILLET OF BEEF

1 (5-6-lbs) fillet of beef
4-5 cloves garlic, slivered
1 teaspoon salt
1 teaspoon pepper
🐷 1 teaspoon Porky's Bellycheer Jalapeño Pepper Sauce
1 cup soy sauce
1 cup port
1 (1/4-inch) piece gingerroot, peeled and grated
1 teaspoon thyme
1 bay leaf
Bacon strips

Cut small gashes in the top of the beef, and fill with the slivers of garlic. Rub the beef with the salt, pepper, and Porky's Bellycheer Jalapeño Pepper Sauce; place the beef in a shallow dish or heavy-duty, self-sealing plastic bag. Combine the soy sauce, port, gingerroot, thyme, and bay leaf in a bowl; mix well. Pour the marinade over the beef, cover the dish or seal the plastic bag, and refrigerate for at least 3 hours or overnight, turning the beef several times.

Remove the beef from the dish or bag, and place it in a shallow roasting pan; discard the marinade. Arrange the strips of bacon over the top of the beef, and bake at 425° for 28 minutes or until a meat thermometer inserted into the thickest part of the fillet registers 140° (for rare) or desired doneness. Remove from the oven; serve hot, at room temperature, or chilled.

"I didn't know what it would do to the players. I made a concerted effort to calm them down. They were as high as I've ever seen. James Joseph is as tough as they come, but I believe he hyperventilated before we came on the field."

–Auburn Coach Pat Dye, on all of the excitement leading up to the historic first-ever meeting between Alabama and Auburn in Jordan-Hare Stadium in 1989.

SUGARBOWL BBQ SHRIMP

8 SERVINGS
1-lb butter, divided
3-4-lbs peeled shrimp
2 tablespoons all-purpose seasoning blend
1 teaspoon chopped garlic
5 oz beer
🐷 1/3 cup Porky's Bellycheer BBQ Seasoning
1 teaspoon lemon juice

Melt 3/4-lb of butter in a large skillet; add the shrimp, seasoning blend and garlic and cook for 2-3 minutes. Stir in the remaining ingredients and cook for 3-6 minutes or until the shrimp are cooked and the sauce thickens. Add the remaining butter and shake the skillet until the butter melts and the mixture becomes creamy. Serve with slices of fresh French bread.

CRUSTY PARMESAN CHICKEN

4-5 SERVINGS

You can easily double or triple this recipe to feed a crowd.

1 cup dry bread crumbs
1/4 cup grated Parmesan cheese
2 tablespoons chopped parsley
1/2 teaspoon garlic salt
1/2 teaspoon paprika
1/4 teaspoon pepper
4 tablespoons butter or margarine, melted
1 (3-lb) chicken cut into pieces (or 3-lbs chicken breasts, legs and/or wings)

Preheat the oven to 350°F. Grease a baking pan.

Combine the breadcrumbs, Parmesan cheese, parsley, garlic salt, papri-ka, salt and pepper in a bowl; stir until well mixed. Pour the melted butter into a shallow dish; dip each piece of chicken into the butter and then into the breadcrumb mixture. Arrange the coated chicken, skin side up and without touching each other, in a lightly greased baking pan; bake at 350° for 1 hour or until the chicken is no longer pink. Remove the chicken from the oven; wrap in foil and keep warm until serving time; or cover loosely and refrigerate to serve cold later.

LEG O' LAMB

SERVES 6 - 8

1 leg of lamb, 4–5-lbs, boned, fat trimmed and butterflied
1 cup dry red wine
1/2 cup olive oil
2 tablespoons balsamic vinegar
1 tablespoon dried thyme
1 tablespoon rosemary
1 tablespoon oregano
1 tablespoon parsley
1/4 teaspoon cayenne pepper
2 cloves garlic, minced
2 large sweet onions, peeled and sliced about 1/4 inch thick

Mix the wine, oil, herbs, spices and garlic in a bowl. Let the mixture set for a few minutes, stirring occasionally.

Place the lamb and onions in a non-aluminum container with a tight-fitting cover. Pour the wine/oil mixture over them and seal the con-tainer. Place in refrigerator overnight or longer–the longer it mari-nates, the more intense the flavor.

Grill the lamb over a medium fire with the grill closed for about 20 minutes, basting once. Turn the lamb, baste and replace grill cover.

Cook for another 20 minutes, basting again halfway through. Grill onions alongside the lamb.

BEER BOILED SHRIMP

This recipe includes homemade cocktail sauce to serve with the cooked shrimp. You can use a bottled sauce if you prefer.

6 cans beer

1-lb kielbasa sausage, cut into 1-inch slices

2-3 bay leaves

1 tablespoon coriander seeds

Salt, pepper to taste

2-lbs large shrimp, rinsed in cold water

🦐 1 cup Porky's Lynchburg Seafood Cocktail Sauce

1 tablespoon freshly squeezed lime juice

Combine the beer, sausage slices, bay leaves, coriander, salt and pepper in a large pot; bring to a boil, reduce the heat and simmer for 10 minutes. Add the shrimp, bring to a boil and boil for 2 minutes or until the shrimp turns pink. Remove from the heat and discard the cooking liquid. Place the shrimp in a serving bowl and either serve hot or cover tightly, refrigerate and serve over ice when chilled with the Porky's Lynchburg Seafood Cocktail Sauce.

RED BEANS, SAUSAGE AND RICE

1 (1-lb) package sage sausage

1 teaspoon vegetable oil

1/2 cup diced smoked ham

1/2 cup chopped onion

1 clove garlic, minced

1/4 teaspoon hot pepper sauce

Salt, pepper to taste

1 medium tomato, diced

2 cups chicken broth

1 cup long-grain enriched rice

1 (16-oz) can red beans, drained

Place the sausage in a skillet and cook over medium heat until brown and crumbly. Remove from the heat and drain; set aside.

Pour the oil into a large, deep skillet with a tight-fitting lid; add the ham, onion and garlic and cook over medium heat for 2-4 minutes. Add the cooked sausage and the remaining ingredients; stir to mix well. Bring the mixture to a boil, reduce heat, cover and simmer 15-20 minutes or until the rice is tender.

Third Down Menu

Chutney-Nut Stuffed Brie (p17)

✕

Spicy Grilled Shrimp Skewers (p52)

✕

Potato Wedges (p42)

✕

Red Cabbage Coleslaw (p34)

✕

Pasta Salad (p35)

✕

Lemon Curd Icebox Pie with Whipped Cream (p81)

✕

Buttermilk Pecan Pralines (p91)

B R U N S W I C K   S T E W

This recipe comes from John Derrick, assistant manager of V. Richard's in the Forest Park area of Birmingham. John shares his great love of food and football in his favorite gameday dish. Cook the day before an early Saturday game. For a later kick-off, start cooking late morning and simmer until serving.

2 large carrots, peeled and diced
2 yellow onions, diced
3 tablespoons butter
2 (14 1/2--oz) cans chicken broth
2 (35-oz) cans peeled tomatoes
2 (14 3/4-oz) cans sweet creamed corn
2 (10-oz) cans Castleberry BBQ pork
2 (10-oz) cans Castleberry BBQ beef
2 (10-oz) cans Castleberry BBQ chicken
4 Idaho potatoes, diced
2 tablespoons Worcestershire sauce
3 tablespoons hot sauce
Salt and pepper to taste

Sauté onions and carrots with the butter in a large stock pot until tender over medium high heat. Add chicken broth and reduce heat to medium low.

Add all the canned items, including juice in cans. Add the Worcestershire and hot pepper sauces along with salt and pepper. Simmer at least 3 hours. Add potatoes 1 hour before serving to prevent over cooking.

John likes to serve this dish with corn chips and says the longer it stews, the better it tastes.

C H I L I   R E C I P E S

H O T   D O G   C H I L I
ENOUGH CHILI FOR 12 HOT DOGS
2 tablespoons butter
1/2 cup chopped onion
2-lbs ground chuck
1 1/2 teaspoons chili powder
1 teaspoon paprika
1/2 teaspoon garlic salt
1/2 teaspoon kosher salt
1/2 teaspoon pepper
1/8 teaspoon crushed red pepper

Melt the butter in a large skillet over medium high heat; add the onion and cook until transparent. Remove the onion and set aside.

Add the ground beef to the skillet and cook until browned and crumbly. Add the cooked onion and cook for an additional 5 minutes. Add the remaining ingredients, reduce the heat and simmer for 2-3 hours. Remove from the heat and serve hot over grilled, boiled, or microwaved hot dogs.

BARKLEY'S BEST CHILI

1/2-lb pinto beans
5 cups canned tomatoes
1/2-lb, green or red peppers, chopped
1 tablespoon canola oil
1 tablespoon butter
1-lb. onion, chopped
4 cloves garlic, chopped
1/2 cup chopped parsley
2-2 1/2-lbs ground beef or chuck
1-lb. lean ground pork
1/3 cup chili powder
2 tablespoons salt
1 1/2 teaspoon pepper
2 teaspoons cumin seed
2 teaspoons Accent seasoning

Wash and drain the beans; place in water and soak overnight. Drain beans and put in a pot with enough water to cover completely. Cook until tender and then add tomatoes and cook for 10 minutes. Sauté the pepper in the olive oil and butter for about 5 minutes and then add onion and garlic. When they are softened, add the parsley. Cook the ground beef until browned; drain and add to the onion mixture. Add the chili powder and cook for 15 minutes. Add the onion/beef mixture to the cooked beans and add the remaining spices. Simmer for another hour, stirring occasionally. Garnish chili with sour cream and sliced jalapeños.

SIRLOIN CHILI

This game day recipe is from Rick Little, owner of V. Richards in the Forest Park area of Birmingham.

5-lbs top sirloin, cubed
3 tiny cubes chorizo sausage
2 bunches green onions
1 poblano pepper
2 large onions
5-6 bell peppers
4 ancho or anaheim dried chilies
1 clove garlic
16-oz tomato juice

"Auburn, Alabama –The New Football Capital of the South"

–Billboard along U.S. 280 in Alexander City prior to the 1989 Alabama-Auburn game in Jordan-Hare Stadium. It was the first time since 1947 the game had not been played in Birmingham's Legion Field.

TAILGATING TIPS

* If you're using a charcoal grill, bring along extra water to douse the embers and a plastic garbage bag to put the cold coals in.

* Food should be ready 90 minutes before the game starts. This leaves plenty of time for those going to the game to eat, clean up and extinguish fires. (Those not going to the game can pull out the generator and TV.)

* Ziploc bags are the greatest invention since sliced bread for the serious tailgater.

* Organize the cooler with drinks on one side and food on the other. Place appetizers on top, so you don't have to dig for the first course.

1 (3-qt) can chili beans
1 (3-qt) can crushed tomatoes
2 bottles dark beer
1/2 pot decaf coffee
1 cup chili powder
1/2 cup cumin
1 tablespoon cayenne pepper
1/4 cup balsamic vinegar
1 tablespoon salt
1 tablespoon pepper

Roast the dried ancho chilies in a very large braising pot with no oil for 10–15 minutes until crisp and smoking; remove and crush. In same pot, add chopped peppers and onions. Cook for 10–15 minutes until they stick to the pot. Then add sausage and meat, cook for 10 minutes. Deglaze pot with dark beer and coffee. Scrape the bottom of the pot to remove black from pot for flavor. Add all seasonings, then add the tomato juice. Next add the tomatoes and finally the beans. Cook over low heat for 45 minutes.

JOEY'S TEXAS CHILI RECIPE
15-20 SERVINGS
3-lbs chicken pieces
1 bunch celery, sliced
1 bunch carrots, sliced
1 sweet onion, chopped
2 bay leaves
1-lb tomatoes, finely chopped
1 (15-oz) can tomato sauce
1/4 cup diced celery
2 tablespoons minced garlic
2 tablespoons sugar
8 to 10-lbs venison or flank steak, cut into 1/2-inch cubes
2-lbs sage pork or other sausage
1 can beer
5-oz chili powder
2 tablespoons oregano
2 tablespoons cumin
2 tablespoons salt
2 tablespoons white pepper
2 tablespoons pepper
2 tablespoons thyme
2 tablespoons cilantro
3 sweet onions, chopped
3 green bell peppers, chopped

Combine the chicken pieces, sliced celery, carrots, onion, and bay leaves in a large stockpot; add enough water to fill the pot three-quarters full. Bring to a boil, reduce heat, and simmer for 2 hours. Remove from the heat, and strain. Reserve the chicken and broth, and discard the cooked celery, carrots, onion, and bay leaves. Remove the skin and bones from the chicken. Cut the meat into chunks, place into containers, cover tightly, and refrigerate. Pour the broth into containers, cover tightly, and refrigerate.

Combine the chopped tomatoes, tomato sauce, chopped celery, garlic, and sugar in a large saucepan over medium heat; simmer for 1 1/2 hours. Remove from the heat; pour into containers, cover tightly, and refrigerate.

Cook the cubed venison or flank steak. Drain and place into containers; cover tightly, and refrigerate.

Place the sausage in a large skillet; cook until browned and crumbly. Drain and place into containers; cover tightly, and refrigerate.

About 3 hours before serving, pour the tomato mixture into a large stockpot over medium-low heat. Add the beer, chili powder, oregano, cumin, salt, white pepper, pepper, thyme, and cilantro; stir to mix well. Add the cooked chicken, chicken broth, cooked venison or flank steak, cooked sausage, 3 chopped onions, and chopped bell peppers; stir to mix. Simmer for at least 2 hours before serving.

SANDWICH RECIPES

ROAST BEEF AND SPINACH ROUNDS

4 SERVINGS

1 (3-oz) package cream cheese, softened

1 tablespoon horseradish

1/4 teaspoon pepper

1 tablespoon milk

1 (13 to 14-inch) flour tortilla or 2 (6 to 8-inch) flour tortillas, at room temperature

1/3 to 1/2-lb very thinly sliced roast beef

2 medium tomatoes, very thinly sliced

6-8 spinach leaves

Beat the cream cheese until light and fluffy in a small bowl. Stir in the horseradish, pepper and enough milk to make the mixture easy to spread.

Lightly moisten both sides of the tortilla with water and lay it flat on a damp paper towel. Spread the cream cheese mixture across the top; add layers of beef, tomatoes and spinach leaves. Roll up the tortilla; wrap in the paper towel and then in plastic wrap. Refrigerate for up to 4 hours; just before serving, cut the roll into 2 to 3-inch pieces.

CHICKEN OPEN SESAME
4 SERVINGS
1 cup mayonnaise or salad dressing
2 tablespoons soy sauce
1 teaspoon white wine vinegar
2 tablespoons toasted sesame seeds
1/4 teaspoon ground ginger
2 cups chopped cooked chicken
1 cup chopped snowpeas
1 cup chopped red bell pepper
1/2 cup almonds
4 whole pita breads, cut in half

Combine the mayonnaise, soy sauce, vinegar, sesame seeds and ginger in a bowl; mix well. Add the chicken, snowpeas, bell pepper and almonds; stir to mix well. Spoon the mixture into the pita pockets.

STUFFED FRENCH LOAF
4-6 SERVINGS
1 (1-lb) loaf French bread
2 cups (about 8-oz) very finely chopped cooked chicken or turkey
2 cups diced ham
4 hard boiled eggs, chopped
1/3 cup finely chopped green onions
1 cup dill pickle relish, drained
6 tablespoons mayonnaise
3 tablespoons capers, drained
2 tablespoons Dijon mustard
2 teaspoons white balsamic vinegar
1 teaspoon Worcestershire sauce
Garlic salt, to taste
Pepper, to taste

Cut a 1 1/2-inch-thick slice off each end of the loaf of bread and set aside. Use a long serrated knife to cut and pull out the soft center of the bread, leaving a shell about 1/2 inch thick; set the bread shell aside.

Combine the chicken, ham, eggs, onions, pickles and parsley in a bowl; stir gently to mix. Combine the mayonnaise, capers, mustard, vinegar, Worcestershire sauce and herbs in a small bowl; mix well and stir into the chicken-ham mixture. Add garlic salt and pepper to taste; stir gently to mix.

Stand the bread shell on end and stuff with the chicken-ham mixture, using a long-handled spoon to pack the filling. Place the stuffed loaf on a sheet of foil and replace the end slices. Wrap the loaf and refrigerate for at least 4 hours; unwrap and cut into 3/4-inch slices. Before serving, cut the loaf into 3/4-inch slices.

MAIN DISH SALAD

LAYERED TACO SALAD

10-12 SERVINGS

Preparation and serving tips: *Queso Fresco is now widely available in the dairy section of most supermarkets; you can use shredded cheddar or Monterey Jack if you prefer. You can make this recipe the day ahead, cover it and refrigerate until serving time. Serve this salad with tortilla chips or topped with thinly sliced, toasted tortillas.*

$1^1/2$ -lbs lean ground beef

2 cloves garlic, minced

1 teaspoon salt

1 teaspoon chili powder

$1/4$ teaspoon cumin

1 (15-oz) can pinto beans, rinsed and drained

2 cups sour cream

$1^1/3$ cups (about 14-oz) salsa

2 tablespoons freshly squeezed lime juice

1 tablespoon olive oil

2 avocados, diced

1 head romaine lettuce, chopped (about 14 cups)

3 cups chopped, seeded tomato

1 cup thinly, vertically sliced red onion

$1/2$ cup chopped cilantro

$1^1/2$ cups Queso Fresco, crumbled

Lime wedges (optional)

Layered Taco Salad

Cook the beef in a large skillet over medium high heat for 6 minutes or until brown and crumbly; drain well and return the meat to the skillet. Add the garlic, salt, chili powder and cumin; cook for 1 minute, stirring frequently. Remove the pan from heat; spoon the mixture into a large bowl and let cool completely. Add the beans; stir well and set aside.

Combine the sour cream and salsa in a small bowl; stir well and set aside.

In another bowl, combine the lime juice and olive oil; stir with a whisk until mixed. Add the avocado and toss gently to coat; set aside.

Place half of the lettuce (about 7 cups) in the bottom of a large serving bowl; top with the meat-bean mixture and remaining lettuce. Spoon the sour cream-salsa mixture evenly over the lettuce; top with the tomato and onion. Spoon the avocado mixture evenly over the tomatoes; top with the chopped cilantro and the Queso Fresco. Cover and refrigerate until serving time; serve with lime wedges, if desired.

SAUCES, RUBS & MARINADES

A true tailgater can never plan too far ahead and we've got just what you need to punch up your main course long before you fire up the grill. Making your own sauce, rub or marinade means extra work, but the payoff at the end is well worth it. Here you'll find a slew of recipes gathered from across the Southeast to make your barbecue a meal to remember on game day. From classic barbecue sauces to tangy basters, from exotic marinades to spicy rubs, you'll find something for whatever's on the grill – beef, pork or poultry.

BASIC ADOBO SAUCE

MAKES 2 CUPS

10 to 12 canned Chipotle chilies, chopped
2 large yellow onions, diced
12 cloves of garlic, chopped
4 to 6 tomatoes, diced
4 tablespoons tomato paste
1 teaspoon dry Mexican oregano
1/2 teaspoon ground cumin
1/2 teaspoon cumin seeds
1/4 cup sugar
1/2 cup cider vinegar
1/2 cup chopped fresh cilantro
4 cups water

Mix ingredients in a medium-sized pot and bring to a boil. Reduce heat and simmer until the liquid has boiled down to half of its original volume, then remove from heat and let cool. Process in a blender until you have a smooth mixture. You can use Adobo Sauce right away, or store in the refrigerator until needed.

SHERRY MARINADE FOR STEAK AND CHICKEN

Marinate steak or chicken in this marinade for at least 1 hour before grilling.

3/4 cup soy sauce
2 tablespoons dry mustard
2 tablespoons salt
11/2 teaspoons parsley
1/2 cup sherry or burgundy

Combine all of the ingredients in a bowl and mix well. Pour the mixture into a jar or other container with a tight lid and refrigerate for up to 4 months.

BARBECUE RUB-A-DOO

ABOUT 3 1/2 CUPS

1 cup paprika
3/4 cup ground ancho chile
1/2 cup coarse salt
1/4 cup firmly packed light brown sugar
1/4 cup granulated sugar
1/4 cup granulated garlic
1/4 cup granulated onion
1/4 cup freshly ground black pepper
2 tablespoons ground cumin

Mix ingredients thoroughly in a large bowl – no other preparation necessary! You can use this rub immediately upon mixing, or store it in an airtight container. Apply the night before for maximum flavor.

NEW ZEALAND LAMB MARINADE

3/4 cup port wine
2 tablespoons olive oil
1 teaspoon dried, minced onion
1 teaspoon dried mint or 1 tablespoon chopped, fresh mint
1/2 teaspoon dried oregano
1/2 teaspoon dried rosemary
1/2 teaspoon ground black pepper
1 or 2 dashes hot sauce

Mix ingredients and let sit overnight.

Vary the ingredients according to your personal tastes, although we suggest keeping the mint in any version you develop.

BOURBON-FLAVORED MARINADE FOR GRILLED MEATS AND VEGETABLES

ABOUT 1 CUP

Try this marinade on all kinds of meats and vegetables.
Mix the marinade ahead of time and store it in the refrigerator in a heavy-duty, self-sealing plastic bag. At least 1 hour before grilling, place your favorite meat and vegetables in the bag and let them marinate until you are ready to cook them.

1 small onion, finely chopped
1 clove garlic, finely chopped
1/3 cup bourbon
1/4 cup soy sauce
1/4 cup brown sugar
1/4 cup mustard
Dash of Worcestershire sauce

Combine all of the ingredients in a bowl and mix well. Pour the marinade into a heavy-duty, self-sealing plastic bag and refrigerate.

GRAND CANYON BASTING SAUCE

1 cup tomato sauce
1 cup chili sauce
1/4 cup steak sauce
1/4 cup dried parsley
3 cloves garlic, minced
2 tablespoons dry mustard
2 tablespoons prepared horseradish
2 tablespoons dark syrup
1 tablespoon Worcestershire sauce
1 tablespoon red wine vinegar
1 teaspoon cayenne pepper

Blend the ingredients to a smooth consistency (a blender may be needed). After all ingredients are well-mixed, let stand for about 15 minutes to let the flavors meld together. This sauce gives a sweet, rich flavor to pork, beef and poultry. Apply directly while grilling.

RED WINE BARBECUE SAUCE

ABOUT 2 CUPS

Brush the sauce on the food every 20 minutes during grilling.

1 cup dry red wine
1/3 cup red wine vinegar
1/4 cup olive oil
3 tablespoons Worcestershire sauce
1 onion, finely chopped

1 tablespoon sugar

1 tablespoon orange zest

2 cloves minced garlic

Combine the wine, vinegar, oil, Worcestershire sauce, onion, sugar and orange zest in a saucepan. Bring the mixture to a boil, reduce the heat and simmer, partially covered, for 25 minutes (the sauce will not thicken while it cooks). Remove the pan from the heat and add the garlic. Store the sauce in the refrigerator.

ROSEMARY MARINADE

2 tablespoons chopped fresh rosemary, or two teaspoons dried rosemary

2 large cloves garlic, minced

1 1/2 teaspoon salt

1 teaspoon freshly ground pepper

Zest of 1 lemon or lime

Mix all ingredients together, until it forms a regular consistency.

If refrigerated, this marinade will keep for up to three days if you use fresh herbs. Makes about 1/4cup — multiply the ingredients accordingly to make more.

WINE MARINADE

5 CUPS

Use red wine for beef and lamb and white wine for poultry or fish.

3 1/2 cups dry red or white wine

1/2 cup olive oil

1 onion, finely chopped

4 tablespoons chopped fresh parsley

2 large cloves garlic, minced

1 tablespoon chopped fresh thyme, rosemary, or tarragon

1 teaspoon salt

1/2 teaspoon freshly ground pepper

Combine all of the ingredients in a large bowl; whisk to blend. You can use the marinade immediately, or store it in a tightly covered container in the refrigerator for up to 2 days.

TAILGATING TIPS

* Mix hearty salads on the spot. Pack chopped vegetables and dressing in the cooler. Add canned meat, seafood or chicken just before serving. Reminder: Pack the can opener.

* Pack up the car the night before with tables, chairs, trash bags and soap, water and towels to wash up with before cooking and eating. Use two insulated coolers–one for drinks and ready-to-eat foods, the other for raw meats. Pack foods in reverse order so the last ones packed will be the first ones used.

YELLOWJACKET BARBECUE SAUCE

1 medium onion, finely minced
4 cloves garlic, finely minced
2 tablespoons olive oil
1 cup cider vinegar
2/3 cup prepared mustard
1/3 cup brown sugar
1 tablespoon ancho chile powder
1 tablespoon paprika
1 teaspoon finely ground black pepper
1/4 tablespoon cayenne
2 tablespoons butter or margarine
Dash of soy or Worcestershire sauce

Sauté the onion and garlic cloves over medium heat in the olive oil.
Cook them just long enough so that they are soft. Add the vinegar,
brown sugar, cayenne, chili powder, paprika and pepper. Bring to a
boil and simmer for 10 minutes.

Add butter/margarine and soy/Worcestershire sauce and remove from
the heat. For a smoother mix, puree before serving. Tastes great with
pork.

BEEHIVE BASTING SAUCE

2 CUPS
1 cup orange juice (fresh if available)
1/4 cup butter
1/2 cup honey
1/4 cup mushroom soy sauce
1/4 cup chopped fresh cilantro or 2 tablespoons dried cilantro
2 tablespoons lemon juice
1 tablespoon dry mustard
1 tablespoon vinegar
1 clove garlic, minced

Mix the ingredients over medium heat until it forms an even consistency. Works well for basting poultry, especially a whole turkey.

OLD HAVANA SAUCE

APPROXIMATELY 1 1/2 CUPS
1/4 cup plus 2 tablespoons vegetable oil
1 medium onion, diced
2 cloves garlic, minced
1 to 2 Scotch bonnet or red jalapeño chilies, seeded and diced
2 roasted red peppers, coarsely chopped
2 tablespoons chopped cilantro

2 bay leaves
2 cups tomato sauce
Coarse salt and freshly ground black pepper to taste
Turbinado or brown sugar and fresh lime juice to taste

Heat the oil in a medium saucepan over medium heat. Sauté onion, garlic and chilies until tender – this should only take 3 to 4 minutes. Add the peppers, cilantro and bay leaves and continue sautéing for 5 more minutes, stirring occasionally. Add tomato sauce and bring the mixture to a boil.

Reduce the heat and simmer for 15 minutes.

Season with salt and pepper, then remove and discard the bay leaves. Puree with a hand blender or food processor until smooth and thick. If you like, try adjusting the flavor to your preference with small amounts of sugar and lime juice.

TAILGATING BARBEQUE SAUCE

1 cup chili sauce
1/2 cup beer
1/3 cup vegetable oil
1/4 cup finely chopped onion
1/4 cup finely chopped cilantro
3 tablespoons chili powder
1 teaspoon ground cumin
1/2 teaspoon dried red pepper
1/4 teaspoon salt
2-lbs (1-inch-thick) flank steak

Combine all of the ingredients except the steak in a medium-size bowl; mix until well blended. Place the steak in a shallow dish or heavy-duty, self-sealing plastic bag; pour the chili-beer mixture over the steak. Either cover the dish tightly or seal the bag and refrigerate for at least 3 hours.

Remove the steak and place on a well-oiled grill; discard the marinade. Cook the steak until desired doneness (25-30 minutes for medium-rare), turning only once. Remove the steak from the grill and cut across the grain into thin slices.

4TH QUARTER
d e s s e r t s

Y ou saved room, right? Read on for the most delectable tailgating desserts. Whether you want a batch of Quarterback Caramel Brownies that'll stay warm on the drive or a Glazed Whiskey Cake to serve up at home, we've included the best way to finish up your tailgating festivities. Cakes, pies and other sweets are here for you to reward those who kept their hands to themselves while you were cooking everything else. What better way to celebrate the latest win than by indulging the old sweet tooth?

Left: Espresso Crunchies, *page 82*

Right: Pumpkin-Walnut Cake, *page 74*

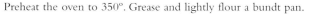

HARVEY WALLBANGER BUNDT CAKE

1 package yellow cake mix
1 (3-oz) package instant vanilla pudding
1/2 cup vegetable oil
4 eggs
1/4 cup vodka
1/4 cup Galliano
1/4 cup orange juice
Confectioners' sugar

Preheat the oven to 350°. Grease and lightly flour a bundt pan.

Combine all of the ingredients except the confectioners' sugar in a large bowl; beat for 4 minutes with an electric mixer. Pour the batter into the prepared pan and bake for 45-50 minutes or until a cake tester comes out clean. Let the cake cool in the pan for 15 minutes; remove from the pan and let cool completely. Just before serving, dust the top of the cake with confectioners' sugar.

PUMPKIN-WALNUT CAKE

ABOUT 12 SERVINGS
11/2 cups sugar
1/2 cup butter, softened
3 eggs, lightly beaten
1 (15-oz) can pumpkin
1 teaspoon vanilla extract
3 cups sifted cake flour
1 teaspoon baking powder
1 teaspoon baking soda
1 teaspoon ground cinnamon
1/2 teaspoon salt
1/4 teaspoon ground ginger
1/4 teaspoon ground nutmeg
1 cup chopped, toasted walnuts
2 tablespoons confectioners' sugar

Preheat the oven to 325°. Coat a 10-inch bundt pan with cooking spray.

Combine the sugar and butter in a large bowl; beat at medium speed with an electric mixer for 5 minutes or until well blended. Add the eggs one at a time, beating well after each addition. Add the pumpkin and vanilla; beat well.

Lightly spoon the flour into dry measuring cups; level with a knife. Combine the flour, baking powder, baking soda, cinnamon, salt, ginger and nutmeg in a medium bowl, stir well with a whisk. Add the flour mixture to the pumpkin mixture and fold in until well mixed. Add the nuts and fold in until well mixed.

Spoon the batter into the prepared pan and bake for 55 minutes or until a wooden pick inserted in the center comes out clean. Remove the pan from the oven and let the cake cool for 10 minutes. Remove the cake from the pan and let it cool completely on a wire rack. Just before serving, dust the top of the cake with the confectioners' sugar.

RUM-FLAVORED-POUND CAKE

1 cup chopped nuts
1 package butter recipe yellow cake mix
1 (3-oz) package instant French vanilla pudding mix
1/2 cup water
1/2 cup oil
1/2 cup light or dark rum
4 eggs
1 cup butter
1/4 cup water
2-oz light or dark rum
1 cup sugar

Preheat the oven to 325°. Sprinkle the nuts in the bottom of a well-greased and lightly floured bundt pan.

Combine the cake mix, pudding mix, 1/2 cup of water, oil and 1/2 cup of rum; mix well. Add the eggs one at a time, beating well after each addition. Pour the batter into the prepared pan and bake for 45–50 minutes or until a cake tester comes out clean. Remove the cake from the oven and let it cool in the pan.

While the cake is baking, combine the butter, 1/4 cup of water, 2-oz of rum and sugar in a saucepan, stirring to mix. Place over medium heat and bring to a boil; reduce the heat and cook until the sugar dissolves, stirring constantly. Remove the pan from the heat. Use a meat fork to poke holes in the cake while it is still in the pan; pour the sauce over the cake. Let the cake stand an additional 30 minutes before removing it from the pan.

CHOCOLATE-CHUNK RED VELVET SHEET CAKE

16 SERVINGS

Chunks of semisweet chocolate and a touch of raspberry add a tasty twist on this classic. Simply omit the chopped chocolate and raspberry preserves if you prefer the original.

3/4 cup butter, softened

2 1/4 cups sugar

3 eggs

2 1/4 teaspoons vanilla extract

4 tablespoons red food coloring

3 cups flour

6 tablespoons of cocoa powder

2 1/4 teaspoons baking soda

3/4 teaspoon salt

1 1/2 cups buttermilk

3 (1-oz) blocks semisweet or bittersweet chocolate coarsely chopped into chunks

1/4 cup seedless raspberry preserves

3 cups confectioners' sugar, sifted

1/2 cup butter, softened

1/4 cup milk

1 teaspoon vanilla

1/2 teaspoon lemon juice

Dash salt

Preheat the oven to 350°. Lightly spray a 13 x 9-inch baking pan with cooking spray.

Combine 3/4 cup butter and the sugar in a large bowl; beat with an electric mixer at medium speed about 5 minutes or until light and fluffy. Add the eggs one at a time, beating well after each addition. Add the vanilla and beat well. Add the food coloring and beat at low speed (to avoid splashing) until well mixed.

Lightly spoon the flour into measuring cups; level with a knife. Combine the flour, cocoa powder, baking soda and salt in a small bowl; stir to mix. Add one-third of the flour mixture to the butter mixture and beat well; add one-third of the buttermilk and beat well. Continue alternately adding the flour and buttermilk, beating well after each addition. Pour the batter into the prepared pan and bake for 50 minutes or until wooden pick inserted in the center comes out clean. Remove the pan from the oven and place on a wire rack; let the cake cool completely in the pan. Spread the preserves in an even layer over the top of the cake; cover tightly and place in the freezer for 15 minutes.

Combine the confectioners' sugar, 1/2 cup butter, 1/4 cup milk, 1 teaspoon vanilla, lemon juice and salt in a medium bowl; beat with an electric mixer at medium speed until smooth and fluffy. Spread the frosting in an even layer over the chilled cake; cover and refrigerate. Serve chilled or at room temperature.

FRESH APPLE CAKE

2 cups sugar
1 1/2 cups vegetable oil
3 cups flour
1 teaspoon salt
1 teaspoon baking soda
1 teaspoon vanilla
2 eggs
3 cups chopped apples
1 cup chopped pecans
Juice of 1/2 lemon
1 cup confectioners' sugar
1/2 teaspoon vanilla
1 tablespoon light corn syrup

Preheat oven to 300. Grease a bundt cake pan.

Combine apples and sugar in a medium size mixing bowl; set aside.

Combine flour, salt and baking soda in another medium size mixing bowl. In a large mixing bowl, mix eggs, oil and vanilla. Beat on medium speed until well mixed. Add the combined dry ingredients and the apple/sugar mixture alternately into the egg mixture. Stir in the pecans. Bake for 1 hour.

For lemon glaze, beat the confectioners' sugar, lemon juice, vanilla and corn syrup until smooth. If needed, add a slight amount of warm water to thin it. Drizzle on warm cake.

CHESS CAKE

1 package yellow cake mix
1/2 cup butter or margarine
1 egg
1 (1-lb) box confectioners' sugar
8-oz cream cheese, softened
3 eggs
1/2 cup chopped pecans or other nuts

Preheat the oven to 350°. Grease a 9 x 13-inch backing pan.

Combine the cake mix, butter and 1 egg in a bowl; mix well and press the batter into the prepared pan. Combine the confectioners' sugar, cream cheese and 3 eggs in another bowl; mix well and spread over the cake batter. Bake for 30 minutes; remove from the oven and let the cake cool in the pan. Cut into serving-size pieces.

COCONUT PINEAPPLE CAKE

24 SERVINGS

2 eggs
2 cups sugar
2 cups crushed pineapple
2 cups flour
2$1/2$ teaspoons baking powder
1 cup sugar
1/2 cup butter
1 (5$1/2$-oz) can evaporated milk
1 cup coconut
1 cup chopped pecans
1 teaspoon vanilla
1/2 teaspoon lemon juice

Preheat the oven to 350°. Grease and flour a 9 x 13-inch baking pan.

Combine the eggs and 2 cups sugar in a large bowl; beat until well mixed. Add the pineapple and stir to mix. Add the flour and baking powder; mix thoroughly. Pour the batter into the prepared pan; bake for 25-30 minutes or until a cake tester comes out clean. Remove the pan from the oven.

Combine 1 cup of sugar, butter and evaporated milk in a saucepan over medium heat; bring to a boil, stirring constantly and cook 3-4 minutes. Remove the pan from the heat and add the coconut, pecans, vanilla and lemon juice; stir to mix well. Poke holes in the top of the hot cake using a toothpick; pour the coconut-pecan mixture over the cake and let it cool.

GLAZED WHISKEY CAKE

You can make this cake up to a week ahead of time and store it in the refrigerator.

1 package white or butter recipe yellow cake mix
1 (3-oz) package instant vanilla or French vanilla pudding mix
1 cup milk
1/2 cup oil
1-oz bourbon whiskey
4 eggs
1 cup finely chopped walnuts or pecans
2 tablespoons flour
1 cup butter
3/4 cup sugar
1/2 cup bourbon whiskey
Confectioners' sugar

Preheat the oven to 350°. Grease and flour a bundt or 10-inch tube pan.

Combine the cake and pudding mixes in a large bowl; stir in the milk, oil and 1-oz of bourbon. Add the eggs one at a time, beating well after each addition. Place the nuts in a small bowl, sprinkle the flour over the nuts and stir to coat; fold the flour-coated nuts into the batter. Pour the batter into the prepared pan and bake for 45-55 minutes or until a cake tester comes out clean. Remove the cake from the oven and let it cool in the pan.

Combine the butter, sugar and 1/2 cup bourbon in a small saucepan; place over medium heat and cook, stirring constantly, until the butter melts and the mixture is bubbly. Remove the pan from the heat. Poke about 8 holes in the top of the cake while it is still in the pan and pour the glaze over cake. Let cake cool in the pan for 2 hours; remove the cake from pan, wrap it in foil and refrigerate for at least 24 hours. Just before serving, dust the top of the cake with confectioners' sugar.

Fourth Down Menu

Cheddar Cheese Dip served with chips and vegetables (p18)

✕

Layered Taco Salad (p65)

✕

Creamy Corn Casserole (p43)

✕

Fan's Favorite Lemon Squares (p84)

✕

Bourbon-Walnut Brownie Bites (p83)

CAMPUS CARROT CAKE

20-24 SERVINGS

2$1/2$ cups flour

2 cups sugar

1 teaspoon cinnamon

$1/2$ teaspoon nutmeg

$1/2$ teaspoon allspice

1 teaspoon salt

$1/2$ teaspoon baking powder

$1/2$ teaspoon baking soda

1 cup vegetable oil

4 eggs

2 cups shredded carrots

$1/2$ cup chopped walnuts (optional)

1 (3-oz) package cream cheese, softened

$1/4$ cup butter or margarine, softened

1 tablespoon milk

1 teaspoon vanilla extract

2 cups confectioners' sugar

Additional chopped walnuts (optional)

Preheat the oven to 350°. Grease a 9 x 13-inch baking pan.

Combine the flour, sugar, cinnamon, nutmeg, allspice, salt, baking powder and baking soda in a large bowl; mix well. Combine the oil and eggs in a small bowl; mix well and add to the flour mixture, stirring until thoroughly mixed. Add the carrots; stir well. Fold in the walnuts, if desired. Pour the batter into the prepared pan and bake for 35-40 minutes or until a cake tester comes out clean. Remove the pan from the oven and let the cake cool.

Combine the cream cheese, butter, milk and vanilla in a bowl; beat until smooth. Add the confectioners' sugar and mix well. Spread the mixture over the top of the cooled cake; sprinkle with chopped walnuts, if desired. Refrigerate until serving time; cut into serving-size pieces.

CHOCOLATE CHESS PIE

1 (8-INCH) PIE

1$1/2$ cups sugar

4 tablespoons cocoa

2 eggs, beaten

1 small can evaporated milk

$1/2$ cup butter, softened

1 teaspoon vanilla

1 (8-inch) unbaked pie shell

Preheat the oven to 350°.

Combine the sugar and cocoa in a large bowl; stir to mix well. Add the eggs, milk, butter and vanilla; mix until well blended. Pour the mixture into the unbaked pie shell and bake for 45 minutes. Remove the pie from the oven and let cool.

LEMON CURD ICEBOX PIE WITH WHIPPED CREAM

12 SERVINGS

Preparation tip: *You can make the Lemon Curd up to 4 days ahead; bake and fill the piecrust the day of the party.*

1 (9-inch) pre-made deep dish piecrust

11/2 cups sugar

3 tablespoons cornstarch

6 egg yolks

1 cup fresh lemon juice

6 tablespoons butter, cut into small pieces

1 cup heavy cream

2 tablespoons confectioners' sugar, sifted

Lemon slices

Lemon Curd Icebox Pie

Bake the piecrust according to package directions for a 1-crust filled pie; remove from the oven and let cool completely.

Combine the sugar and cornstarch in a bowl; stir with a whisk to mix. Add the egg yolks and whisk until smooth; add the lemon juice and whisk until blended. Spoon the mixture into a saucepan; add the butter and cook over medium heat until the butter melts, stirring often. Increase the heat to medium high and bring the mixture to a boil, stirring constantly; cook for 1 minute or until the mixture becomes thick, stirring constantly. Remove the pan from heat and spoon the curd into a glass bowl; let cool to room temperature.

After the curd has cooled, gently whisk it until smooth. Spoon the curd into the baked piecrust; cover lightly with plastic wrap and refrigerate until it is completely chilled (the mixture will thicken as it cools). About 30 minutes before serving, place the heavy cream and sifted confectioners' sugar in a large bowl; beat with an electric mixer at medium high speed just until medium peaks form. Spread the whipped cream evenly over curd. Garnish with lemon slices.

ESPRESSO CRUNCHIES

1 stick unsalted butter, softened

3 tablespoons sugar

1 cup flour

2-oz bittersweet chocolate, grated

1 cup ground or chopped hazelnuts

1 heaping tablespoon instant coffee

1 tablespoon hot water

Toasted hazelnuts, chopped

Preheat oven to 325°. Combine the butter and sugar. Add the flour, chocolate and chopped hazelnuts. Add water to the coffee and stir; add to the mixture. Shape the mixture into balls and place on an ungreased cookie sheet. Place chopped hazelnuts into the center of each ball; lightly press into the dough. Bake for about 15 minutes.

BANANA BARS

ABOUT 24 SERVINGS

3/4 cup butter, softened

2/3 cup sugar

2/3 cup brown sugar

1 egg, beaten

1 teaspoon vanilla extract

1 cup mashed banana

13/4 cups flour

2 teaspoons baking powder

1/2 teaspoon salt

1 cup semisweet chocolate morsels

1/2 cup confectioner's sugar

Preheat the oven to 350°. Grease and flour a 10 x 15-inch baking (jellyroll) pan.

Combine the butter, sugar and brown sugar in a large bowl; cream until fluffy. Add the egg and vanilla; beat to mix. Fold in the mashed banana.

Combine the flour, baking powder and salt in a small bowl; mix well. Add to the banana mixture, folding to blend. Stir in the chocolate morsels and spread in the prepared pan. Bake for 20 minutes; remove the pan from the oven and let cool. Sprinkle with confectioner's sugar and cut into small squares.

QUARTERBACK CARAMEL BROWNIES

1 package German chocolate cake mix
3/4 cup butter or margarine, melted
1/3 cup evaporated milk
1 cup chopped nuts, optional
1/2 container caramel fruit dip
1 cup chocolate morsels or mini-chips

Preheat the oven to 350°. Grease and flour a 9 x 13-inch baking pan.

Combine the cake mix, butter, milk and nuts in a large bowl; stir until the mixture holds together. Press half of the mixture into the prepared pan and bake for 6 minutes. Remove the pan from the oven and let stand for 1-2 minutes.

Warm the caramel dip in the microwave until soft. Spread the softened caramel over the top of the hot brownie layer; sprinkle the chocolate chips over the caramel and top with the remaining brownie mixture. Bake for an additional 15-18 minutes; remove the pan from the oven and let the brownies cool. Cut into serving-size squares.

BOURBON-WALNUT BROWNIE BITES

24 COOKIES
9 graham crackers, finely ground (about 1 cup)
1/2 cup confectioners' sugar
1/2 cup chopped walnuts
1 tablespoon cocoa powder
Dash salt
2 tablespoons bourbon
2 teaspoons honey
1/2 teaspoon vanilla
1 tablespoon confectioners' sugar
1 teaspoon cocoa powder
24 walnut pieces, toasted

Combine the graham crackers, confectioners' sugar, chopped walnuts, cocoa powder and salt in a bowl; stir to mix. In another bowl, combine the bourbon, honey and vanilla; mix well and drizzle the mixture over the graham cracker mixture, tossing with a fork until combined. Knead the mixture by hand until it forms a very stiff dough (add 1/4 teaspoon hot water if the mixture seems too dry). Divide the dough into 24 balls and place them on a large platter; cover tightly with plastic wrap and let stand at room temperature overnight.

Combine 1 tablespoon of confectioners' sugar with 1 teaspoon of cocoa powder in a large bowl; toss the bourbon balls in the sugar-cocoa mixture and arrange them on a serving tray or dish. Press a walnut piece into the surface of each ball to form a slightly rounded cookie.

FAN'S FAVORITE LEMON SQUARES

32 SQUARES

1 cup butter

1/2 cup confectioners' sugar

1/8 teaspoon salt

21/4 cups flour, divided

4 eggs

2 cups sugar

3 tablespoons freshly squeezed lemon juice

2 tablespoons freshly squeezed lime juice

1 teaspoon finely grated lemon rind

1/2 teaspoon finely grated lime rind

1 teaspoon baking powder

1 tablespoon confectioners' sugar

Preheat the oven to 350°. Lightly coat a 13 x 9-inch baking pan with cooking spray.

Combine the butter, 1/2 cup confectioners' sugar and salt in a bowl; beat with an electric mixer at medium speed for 2 minutes or until fluffy.

Lightly spoon the flour into measuring cups; level with a knife. Add 2 cups of the flour to the butter mixture; beat just until combined. Press the mixture into the prepared pan and bake for 20 minutes or until very lightly browned. Remove the pan from the oven and place it on a rack to cool.

Combine the eggs and sugar in a bowl; beat with an electric mixer at medium high speed for 5 minutes or until the mixture is thick and pale. Add the lemon juice, lime juice, lemon rind and lime rind; beat until well mixed. Combine the remaining 1/4 cup flour and the baking powder; stir with a whisk to mix. Add the flour mixture to the egg mixture; beat until smooth.

Spoon the mixture onto the cooled crust in the pan; return the pan to the oven and bake for 20 minutes or until the top is light brown and the filling is set. Remove the pan from the oven and place it on a wire rack; sprinkle the tablespoon of confectioners' sugar evenly over the top. Let cool completely; cover the pan and refrigerate overnight. Before serving, cut into 32 squares; serve chilled or at room temperature.

SUPER SHORTBREAD COOKIES

32 COOKIES

You may know these cookies as "sand tarts" or "pecan sandies." You can make them several days ahead and store them in an airtight container.

1 cup butter, softened

3/4 cup confectioners' sugar

1 teaspoon vanilla extract

1/8 teaspoon salt

1 cup ground pecans

2 cups flour, divided

1/4 cup confectioners' sugar (optional)

Preheat the oven to 350°.

Combine the butter and 3/4 cup confectioners' sugar in a large bowl; beat with an electric mixer at medium speed for 5 minutes or until very well blended and light in color. Add the vanilla and salt; beat well. Add the ground pecans and continue beating until combined.

Lightly spoon the flour into measuring cups; level with a knife. Add the flour to the butter-sugar mixture and stir by hand until well mixed (the mixture will be very stiff). Spoon the dough onto a sheet of plastic wrap, wrap tightly and refrigerate for at least 1 hour.

Cut the dough into 32 pieces and roll each piece into a ball. Place each ball on an ungreased baking pan and press lightly with the heel of your hand to form a 2-inch cookie, spacing the cookies at least 1/2 inch apart. Bake for 10 minutes or until the cookies are lightly browned on the bottom and dry on the top. Remove the pan from the oven and let the cookies cool on wire racks. When the cookies are completely cool, toss them in confectioners' sugar, if desired.

Linebacker Martavius Houston had just stripped Alabama fullback Ed Scissum of the football, giving the Tigers possession and new life with less than a minute to go in the 1997 Auburn-Alabama game. Now, AU place-kicker Jaret Holmes was lining up for a 39-year-old field goal that would give Auburn a come-from-behind 18-17 victory. Along the sidelines, many of the Auburn players couldn't bear to watch. On the field, Holmes said a prayer. Alabama called two timeouts to try to ice him. Instead, it just made Holmes more confident. He drilled the kick high and down the middle. And then he fell to his knees and looked up at the sky. "I was praying the whole time," Holmes said after the game. A calm, easy feeling came over me. I knew it was going in." Coach Terry Bowden ran onto the field and gave Holmes a big hug. "He has been one of the most valuable players on our team," Bowden said. "He said in the paper you have to win the big one in the last second to be famous around here. Jaret Holmes will be famous around Auburn the rest of his life." Holmes said he was never nervous about the kick. "The Lord up above was taking care of me. He came through for me in the end." But on the last play of the game, when Alabama's A.J. Diaz ran onto the field to try an improbable 57-yard field goal that would give Alabama the victory, Holmes confessed, "I was hoping the Lord wasn't looking after him."

Clockwise from top left: Chocolate Chunk Red Velvet Sheet Cake, *page 76*; Fan's Favorite Lemon Squares *page 84* and Bourbon-Walnut Brownie Bites *page 83*; Minted Pick-Me-Up Iced Tea, *page 9* and Super Shortbread Cookies, *page 85*; Almond Bars, *page 87*

WAR EAGLE® FRUIT BARS

You can substitute other fruit jams like strawberry or blackberry for variation.

2 cups butter, softened

2 cups sugar

4 egg yolks

4 cups flour

1 1/2 cups raspberry jam

Preheat the oven to 350°. Grease a 9 x 13-inch baking pan.

Combine the butter and sugar in a bowl; cream until light and fluffy. Add the egg yolks; blend well. Gradually add the flour, mixing well after each addition. Press half of the dough into the bottom of the prepared pan; spread the jam over the top. Flatten the remaining dough and place it on top of the jam.

Bake for 30 minutes or until the top is lightly browned. Remove the pan from the oven; let cool before cutting into serving-size pieces.

ALMOND BARS

32 COOKIES

You can make this recipe several days ahead and store the cookies in an airtight container.

1 cup butter, softened
1/2 cup sugar
1/2 cup brown sugar
1 teaspoon vanilla
1 large egg, separated
2 cups flour
1/2 teaspoon cinnamon
1/4 teaspoon salt, divided
11/2 cups sliced, blanched almonds
1 tablespoon turbinado or coarse sugar (optional)

Preheat the oven to 325°.

Combine the butter and sugars in a large bowl and beat with an electric mixer at medium speed for 5 minutes or until very well blended and light in color. Add the vanilla and egg yolk and beat well.

Lightly spoon the flour into measuring cups; level with a knife. Combine the flour, cinnamon and 1/8 teaspoon salt in a small bowl; stir to mix. Add the flour mixture to the butter mixture; beat just until combined. Use a stiff spatula or your hands very lightly dipped in water to spread the mixture evenly in a 10 x 15-inch baking pan. Sprinkle the sliced almonds in an even layer over the top and press them into the batter.

Beat the egg white with a fork until foamy and brush it over the almonds. Sprinkle the remaining 1/8 teaspoon salt and the turbinado sugar (if desired) evenly over the top. Bake for 25 minutes or until golden brown; remove the pan from the oven, place on a wire rack, let cool for 5 minutes and cut into 32 serving-size bars while still warm. Remove the bars from the pan and let cool completely on a wire rack.

CHARMING CHOCOLATE

15-20 SERVINGS

2 cups confectioners' sugar
4 tablespoons cocoa
1/4 teaspoon salt
1/2 cup margarine, softened
2 egg yolks
1 cup pecans
1 teaspoon vanilla
2 egg whites, beaten
1 1/4 cups vanilla wafer crumbs, divided
Whipped cream (optional)

Sift the confectioners' sugar into a bowl and measure again. Combine the sifted sugar, cocoa and salt in the sifter; sift into a clean bowl. Add the margarine and cream until light and fluffy. Add the egg yolks one at a time, beating well after each addition. Add the pecans and vanilla; blend well. Fold in the beaten egg whites and set the mixture aside.

Line a 9 x 13-inch pan with waxed paper, letting the waxed paper extend over the sides of the pan. Spread half of the vanilla wafer crumbs in the pan; pour the cocoa-pecan mixture over the layer of crumbs and top with the remaining crumbs. Cover and refrigerate for at least several hours before serving; cut into pieces and serve with whipped cream, if desired.

FANTASTIC FUDGE TORTE

10 SERVINGS

Unsweetened cocoa
1 teaspoon instant coffee powder or granules
2 tablespoons hot water
4-oz semisweet chocolate, melted
3 eggs, separated
1/2 cup butter or margarine
3/4 cup sugar
2-oz almond paste, crumbled or shredded
1/2 cup flour
4-oz semisweet chocolate
1 tablespoon butter or margarine

Preheat the oven to 350°. Grease an 8-inch round cake pan and dust with unsweetened cocoa.

Combine the instant coffee and hot water in a bowl; stir until the coffee dissolves. Add the melted chocolate and stir to mix.

In another bowl, beat the egg whites just until stiff, moist peaks form.

In a third bowl, combine the butter and sugar and cream until light and fluffy. Add the almond paste, egg yolks, coffee-chocolate mixture and flour; beat until well mixed. Add the beaten egg whites one-third at a time, folding in just until blended.

Spread the mixture into the prepared pan and bake for 30 minutes or until lightly browned (be careful not to overbake). Remove the pan from the oven and let the cake cool in the pan for 10 minutes. Remove the from the pan and let it cool completely.

Combine the 4-oz of chocolate and 1 tablespoon of butter in the top of a double boiler; cook over barely simmering water until just melted. Spread the mixture over the top and sides of the cooled cake and let stand for 2-4 hours at room temperature or 10-15 minutes in the refrigerator until the glaze hardens. Serve the torte at room temperature.

VERY BERRY DESSERT

ABOUT 28 SERVINGS

1/2 cup butter, melted

2 cups sugar, divided

36 graham crackers, crushed

4 eggs

2 (8-oz) packages cream cheese, softened

1 teaspoon almond extract

2 (21-oz) cans blueberry or cherry pie filling

1 (16-oz) container frozen whipped topping, thawed

1/2 cup sliced almonds

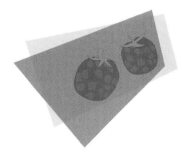

Preheat the oven to 325 °.

Combine the melted butter, 1 cup of sugar and the crushed graham crackers in a bowl; mix well and press into a 9 x 13-inch baking pan.

In a separate bowl, beat the eggs until foamy. Gradually add the cream cheese, remaining 1 cup of sugar and almond extract, beating well after each addition. Pour the mixture over the graham cracker crust and bake for 15-20 minutes. Remove the pan from the oven and let cool.

Pour the pie filling over the top of the baked dessert and top with the whipped topping. Sprinkle with sliced almonds. Refrigerate until ready to serve; cut into serving-size squares.

FRUITY PIZZA

1/2 cup butter, softened
3/4 cup sugar
1 egg
1 1/4 cups flour
1 teaspoon cream of tartar
1/2 teaspoon baking soda
1/4 teaspoon salt
1 (8-oz) package cream cheese, softened
1/2 cup sugar
2 teaspoons vanilla extract
Fresh strawberries, blueberries, kiwi, or other favorite fruit

GLAZE:
1 cup sugar
3 tablespoons cornstarch
dash of salt
3/4 cup water
1 cup orange juice
1/4 cup lemon juice

Preheat the oven to 350°.

Combine the butter and 3/4 cup of sugar in a large bowl; cream until light and fluffy. Add the egg and mix well. Add the flour cream of tartar, baking soda and salt; mix well. Press the mixture onto an ungreased pizza or baking pan. Bake for 8–10 minutes or until lightly browned; remove the pan from the oven and let the crust cool.

Combine the cream cheese, 1/2 cup of sugar and vanilla in a bowl; beat until smooth and spread over the baked crust. Arrange fruit on crust and set aside.

Mix sugar, cornstarch and salt; add water, orange juice and lemon juice in saucepan. Bring to a boil; cook 1 minute until slightly thickened. Cool. Pour over fruit and place the pizza in refrigerator until ready to serve.

APPLE ENCHILADA DESSERT

6 LARGE OR 12 SMALLER SERVINGS

1 (21-oz) can apple pie filling

6 (8-inch) flour tortillas

1 teaspoon ground cinnamon

1/3 cup margarine

1/2 cup sugar

1/2 cup packed brown sugar

1/2 cup water

1 cup chopped nuts

Preheat the oven to 350°. Lightly grease an 8 x 8-inch baking pan.

Spoon one-sixth of the pie filling onto each tortilla and sprinkle with cinnamon. Roll up the tortillas and place seam side down in the prepared pan; set aside.

Combine the margarine, sugar, brown sugar and water in a medium saucepan; place over medium heat and bring to a boil, stirring constantly. Reduce the heat and simmer, stirring constantly, for 3 minutes. Pour the mixture evenly over the filled tortillas; bake for 20 minutes. Remove the pan from the oven and sprinkle with chopped nuts. Cool and serve either whole or cut in half.

BUTTERMILK-PECAN PRALINES

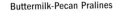
Buttermilk-Pecan Pralines

18 PRALINES

11/2 cups sugar

1/4 cup packed brown sugar

1/2 cup buttermilk

1/2 teaspoon baking soda

Dash salt

1 cup chopped pecans, toasted

2 tablespoons butter

1 teaspoon vanilla extract

Combine the sugar, brown sugar, buttermilk, baking soda and salt in a large saucepan; cook over medium heat until the sugars dissolve, stirring constantly. Continue to cook the mixture over medium heat until a candy thermometer registers 234° (about 8 minutes), stirring occasionally; remove from the heat. Stir in the pecans, butter and vanilla and beat with a wooden spoon until the mixture begins to lose its shine (about 4 minutes). Drop by tablespoonfuls onto waxed paper and let stand for 20 minutes or until set.

RUM BALLS

These are better made up to 5 days ahead; store the rum balls in an airtight container in the refrigerator to allow the flavors to mingle.

1 cup semisweet chocolate morsels
1 cup confectioners' sugar, divided
3 tablespoons light corn syrup
1/2 cup dark rum
21/2 cups vanilla wafer crumbs
1 cup toasted pecans, finely chopped

Preheat the oven to 350°. Spread the pecans on a baking sheet and put in the oven on the center rack for 8 minutes. Allow to cool completely. Finely chop them or process in a food processor until chopped, but not reduced to paste. Process vanilla wafer cookies the same way.

Place the chocolate morsels into the top of a double boiler; place over boiling water and cook until melted, stirring until smooth. Remove the pan from the heat and add 1/2 cup of the confectioners' sugar, the corn syrup and the rum; whisk until smooth.

Combine the vanilla wafer crumbs and pecans in a bowl; stir to mix. Add the chocolate-rum mixture and stir until well blended; shape into 1-inch balls. Place the remaining confectioners' sugar in a shallow dish; roll each of the balls in the sugar and place either on a serving plate or in an airtight container. Cover and refrigerate overnight.

CHOCOLATE-COVERED PRETZELS

1/2 cup slivered almonds
1 (111/2-oz) package milk chocolate morsels
2 tablespoons butter or margarine
30-40 twisted pretzels

Process the almonds in food processor until chopped. Combine the chocolate morsels and butter in the top of a double boiler; cook over boiling water until melted, stirring constantly until the mixture is smooth; add the almonds. Remove the double boiler from the heat, but keep the top over the hot water. Dip the pretzels into the chocolate mixture. Shake off the excess chocolate mixture and place the coated pretzels on a wax paper-lined pan or tray. Chill the coated pretzels for about 30 minutes or until the chocolate sets.

APPLE DIP
2 (8-oz) packages cream cheese
1 cup brown sugar
1 tablespoon vanilla extract
11/2 cup brickle bits
6 granny smith apples, sliced
1/2 cup orange juice

Combine cream cheese, brown sugar and vanilla in a large bowl. Mix well until all of the brown sugar has been blended into the cream cheese and vanilla. Fold in the brickle bits. Refrigerate in a covered container until serving time.

Slice the apples into wedges. Place in a large bowl and toss with the orange juice to prevent browning. Store the apples in a self-sealing, heavy duty plastic bag for transport to tailgate. Serve the dip at room temperature with the apples arranged around the dip bowl.

ZESTY STRAWBERRIES
1/4 cup sugar
1/4 cup orange juice
2 tablespoons dark rum
11/2 teaspoon chopped orange zest
2 pints small strawberries

Combine the sugar, orange juice and rum in a large heavy-duty, self-sealing plastic bag. Add the orange zest and strawberries; seal the bag and refrigerate 2-4 hours, turning the bag twice. To serve, spoon the strawberries and orange-rum juice into dessert glasses at home or small plastic cups at your tailgate.

TAILGATE CHOCOLATE FONDUE
6 SERVINGS
16-oz semisweet chocolate, coarsely chopped
11/2 cups heavy cream
Chunks of fruit, cubes of cake and/or other foods for dipping

Combine the chocolate and heavy cream in a saucepan over very low heat; cook, stirring constantly, until the chocolate melts and blends with the cream. Either serve immediately with the fruit, cake and/or other foods for dipping; or let the mixture cool, refrigerate and reheat when ready to serve.

RESOURCES

INGREDIENTS

Porky's Gourmet Foods
800/PORK911
Bellycheer and Historic Lynchburg
products
www.porkysgourmet.com

Look for the 🐷 symbol
throughout the book for
Porky's products, then log on
or give us a call!

Mention *Eat, Drink & War
Eagle!* in gift message section
of web order, or when you
place an order by phone and
receive a 10% discount.

Coyote Cafe General Store
800/866-4695
Dried chiles, chipotles in
adobo sauce, masa harina
and other spices

Dean & Deluca
800/221-7714
dean-deluca.com
Chile powders, dried
chiles, beans and other
spices

Melissa's Specialty Foods
800/588-0151
melissas.com
Dried chiles, epazote,
piloncillo, tamarind

Penzey's Spice House, Ltd.
800/741-7787
penzeys.com
Chile powders, dried chiles
and epazote

LUMP HARDWOOD

Hasty-Bake
800/426-6836
hastybake.com

SMOKING PELLETS

BBQr's Delight, Inc.
870/535-2247
bbqrsdelight.com

BULLET SMOKERS

Masterbuilt Mfg., Inc.
800/489-1581
masterbuilt.com

PUBLICATIONS

National Barbecue News
barbecuenews.com

WOOD CHUNKS & CHIPS

Sam's Smoker Pro
262/673-0677

SPECIAL THANKS

V. Richards
3916 Clairmont Road
Birmingham, Alabama
205/591-7000
Rick Little, owner of V. Richards
John Derrick, assistant manager

Enjoy Rick's Sirloin Chili
recipe on page 61 and John's
Brunswick Stew recipe on
page 60. Be sure to stop in to
see their new expanded mar-
ket in the Forest Park area of
Birmingham.

**Visit our website to submit recipes for the next edition or to order
additional books: www.eatdrinkandwareagle.com**